For your reading pleasure

YORKSHIRE'S
STRANGEST
TALES

Other titles in the STRANGEST series

The Ashes' Strangest Moments
Boxing's Strangest Moments
Bridge's Strangest Hands
Cinema's Strangest Moments
Classical Music's Strangest Concerts
Cricket's Strangest Moments
Fishing's Strangest Days
Flying's Strangest Moments
Football's Strangest Matches
Gambling's Strangest Moments
Golf's Strangest Rounds
Horse-racing's Strangest Races
Law's Strangest Cases
London's Strangest Tales
Medicine's Strangest Cases
The Military's Strangest Campaigns
Motor-racing's Strangest Races
The Olympics' Strangest Moments
Poker's Strangest Hands
Politics' Strangest Characters
Railways' Strangest Journeys
Rock 'n' Roll's Strangest Moments
Royalty's Strangest Characters
Rugby's Strangest Matches
Sailing's Strangest Moments
Science's Strangest Inventions
Shooting's Strangest Days
Television's Strangest Moments
Tennis's Strangest Matches
Theatre's Strangest Acts
World Cup's Strangest Moments
Kent's Strangest Tales
London Underground's Strangest Tales

For your reading pleasure

YORKSHIRE'S
STRANGEST
TALES

EXTRAORDINARY
BUT TRUE STORIES

A VERY CURIOUS HISTORY

LEONORA RUSTAMOVA

PORTICO

First published in the United Kingdom in 2013 by
Portico Books
10 Southcombe Street
London
W14 0RA

An imprint of Anova Books Company Ltd

ISBN 9781907554919

A CIP catalogue record for this book is available from the British Library.

10 9 8 7 6 5 4 3 2 1

Printed and bound by 1010 Printing International Ltd, China

This book can be ordered direct from the publisher at
www.anovabooks.com

CONTENTS

'There's nowt so queer as folk.'

INTRODUCTION

I'd like to think Yorkshire needs no introduction, but many of the visitors who flock to make its acquaintance still seem remarkably unprepared! The tourist industry here is worth around £7 billion a year, and the county boasts both Britain's first seaside resort, at Scarborough, and the oldest recorded visitor attraction: Mother Shipton's Petrifying Well in Knaresborough. Disneyland it is not, but around 22 million tourist trips per annum to the county is equivalent to the headcount for fun-seekers visiting Walt Disney theme parks worldwide. During the course of writing this book, I have become a walking encyclopedia of Yorkshire-related trivia. I am no historian, but a Yorkshire woman born and bred, with a heart like a Tardis, full of Pennine hills, impenetrable faces, waterfalls, mill ruins, market towns, and soft barn light.

My youth was spent in the countryside, *subjected* to the enthusiasm of my parents' love of local history: a breakfast table littered with flint tools and old clay pipes, long days traipsing over the moors to admire random Roman lumps, and hours of 'fun' in museums and second-hand markets from which my father lugged home air-raid sirens, weaving looms, maps, mouldering books, and still more clay pipes. As a sullen teenager, I liked to think it was boring; the history of my county was just regular background noise at home, along with *The Archers*. I can't believe how much of it stuck, and how it has become so exciting and meaningful since my childhood settled into history as well.

There is nothing simple about Yorkshire, beyond the indisputable softness of a glass of local tap water, or the Arthurian majesty of its mystical autumn sunrises. Even the boundaries require some explanation, as the discrepancy between their position in cartographic terms and their position in the Yorkshire soul is at variance. It was originally three Ridings – the North, East and West (notice the traditional rejection of anything 'South' related) – derived from the old Norse word for 'thirdings'. For all sorts of political reasons, which we like to associate with a nether-county fear of our vastness, there have been a number of periodic reforms to subdivide Yorkshire, although its status as a whole territory remains intact, geographically, culturally and in the media. The Local Government Act of 1972 was a great source of controversy, taking away the Ridings' status. However, by 1996, the East Riding was reinstated, and although some original parts of Yorkshire are still adrift at the edges, it remains by far the largest county in the realm. When relating events from the county therefore, there are times when an area which is no longer within the boundaries is included. Like many Yorkshire people today, I regard the historic boundaries as the true ones and the modern political map-scribblings as a temporary aberration.

The county has provided the stage for many pivotal events in the history of Britain. The Parisii and the Brigantes, the Celtic tribe known as the most militant in Britain, were among its earliest communities. In AD 71 they were eventually conquered by the Romans, who made York (Eboracum) their British capital; during the last two years of Emperor Septimius Severus' life, the entire Roman Empire was run from York. After the Romans, the Celts had a revival and West Yorkshire survived as the last Celtic Kingdom of Elmet until the early seventh century. Then in 866 the Great Heathen Army invaded and the Danes took over York, making it their capital, Jorvik. The area flourished, despite the wild ways of leader Eric Bloodaxe, and trade links were established with northwest Europe, the Mediterranean and the Middle East – a harbinger of the immensely multicultural Yorkshire we have today, where it is a common sight to see an elderly Asian woman in shalwar kameez, cardie and trainers saying, "Ere, I'll give you a hand, luv' to a young, modern man as he struggles to board a bus, complete with toddlers, a buggy and ten bags of shopping.

After a spell with bloodthirsty Bloodaxe in charge, the 'Yorkies' were quite relieved to accept English sovereignty, although when this happened the Kings of England appeared to accept that things were done 'the Norse way' in Yorkshire and they left it to run itself, in the hands of local aristocrats. This independent trait seems to be one that has lived on in the personality of the county, but more on that later. Everyone knows the date of the Battle of Hastings (it is the standard four-digit security code for just about every staffroom door in the land), when William the Conqueror was almost certainly aided to his southern victory by the weariness of Harold II and his soldiers, who had to hurry back from the Battle of Stamford Bridge, where Harald Hardrada of Norway had tried to take over the North. This would all have been so much simpler if they hadn't all been called Harry; the odd Kevin would have made for some clarity. Anyway, Harald was defeated at Hastings, resulting in the Norman conquest of Britain, which the people of Yorkshire didn't take kindly to at all. They fought back in 1069 and rather than let them reclaim York, the Normans burned it to the ground. This began William's awful decree of retribution: the Harrying of the North, in which a vast number of the population north of the Humber perished. It was a cowardly attack, involving a period of indiscriminate murders and much worse: the total decimation of crops and livestock between York and Durham, the burning of villages and destruction of farm tools. The northern people were left to perish from hunger in the winter cold. All that before the Wars of the Roses, the English Civil War, and the rise and fall of the Industrial Revolution!

Much of this historical action seems to have set the Yorkshire temperament as both independent and vaguely disdainful. It is commonly regarded from beyond the county's boundaries as forbidding, outspoken and dour, but Yorkshire folk are quick to find amusement in each other and in themselves. If you are planning on moving to the county, a word to the wise – you have to be able to 'tek it' as well as 'give it' when it comes to humour. Understanding this cultural point could cut down the acceptance period for a newly arrived 'comer-in' by as much as a generation. If you understand the humour, people might begin to accept your grandchildren, or even your children, as locals! Further advice might include avoiding any sign of anticipation, as this is more than likely to retard the process. Yorkshire people do not like to be committed to someone else's expectation. When asked to do something, the closest one can expect to acquiescence is 'aye, mebbe', which is the nearest Yorkshire equivalent to a straightforward yes.

Still, the Yorkshire character is firm, and rises to appreciate anything truly spirited. I grew up in an old vicarage where a previous vicar, a 'comer-in', had struggled to increase his congregation until he responded to the local character. His appeal increased after a visitor to the vicarage demanded of the gardener whether 't'old bugger' was at home. 'Aye, mebbe', was the response, and the visitor proceeded to the vicarage to find that 'the gardener' had got there before him and was in fact 't'old bugger', the vicar himself. This was then consolidated by his losing patience one day with a farmer of the parish who refused to come to the Sunday service and offered to fight him for it. After the vicar had knocked the farmer to the ground (he had boxed for his House at University), he found his church well-attended by those who appreciated a bit of non-verbal communication.

Although the Industrial Revolution had a great impact on the county, with its attendant mass migration of agricultural workers to the towns and cities to find work, we have never really escaped our rural roots. A third of all Britain's National Park area is in Yorkshire, with the Dales, the North York Moors and part of the Peak District, and Leeds, the country's fastest-growing city, is still two-thirds green belt, making it one of Europe's greenest cities, along with neighbouring Sheffield. This close proximity to the natural elements has enhanced the grit of the Yorkshire personality, as I know to my cost from growing up here. At the age of six I was following my parents through a blizzard with a sledge of provisions, and could hardly keep my feet in the deep snow. At the end of my energy I stopped, as did my brother, thinking we couldn't possibly go another step, until my father came back to deliver one of his lectures, the grand finale of which was, 'You have to understand that you are lucky, you kids. There are people all over Britain who don't know what it means to battle with the elements!' He beamed at us through the icicles forming on his face, and we, being such lucky Yorkshire kids, got up and carried on.

When our young local writer, Emily Brontë, wrote her only novel, she took the precaution of submitting it in the name of a man (Ellis Bell), and yet *Wuthering Heights* shocked the genteel literary world in the capital. Acknowledging the 'rugged power' contained in every chapter, the *Atlas* review said, 'We know nothing in the whole range of our fictitious literature, which represents such shocking pictures of the worst forms of humanity.' They'd obviously never hung out in Haworth. There are Cathys and Heathcliffes, and vinegar-faced Josephs, all over Yorkshire to this day. There are feuds which last for generations, and passionate devoted loves, and there are families with Viking surnames living on the hillsides they've lived on for hundreds of years. We may appear rough in our opinions, which are forthright, and our ways, which are impassioned and eccentric, but Humbert Wolfe sums it up in a poem where he remarks to London that, 'York was a capital city when you were just a nameless stew.'

The determination of the Yorkshire spirit is as evident in the county's immeasurable contribution to science and progress as in its refusal to change in its essence. I have endeavoured to capture some of that essence in my choice of entries for this book: from brave pioneers to visionary engineers; inspired troublemakers to grand-scale bakers; with a bit of prehistory for good measure. I hope this book entertains as much as I was entertained in researching it, and as much as my household were exasperated by my endlessly going on about it.

With my love and thanks to Yorkshire's strangest friends, who 'helped' such a lot, turning up while I was writing and saying things like, 'I remember once going across this really old wooden bridge ... I can't remember where, but there must be a story behind it.' In particular James Mason, Rosie Duke and Paul Correy, who provided me so much mirth and practical assistance. To my daughter Flora, who offers me a perspective on how unmoved I was by history at her age, and to Jono Gale, likewise, who insisted on distracting me when I needed it most. Above all, I would like to thank my parents, Chris and Lois Huck, who made Yorkshire the first thing I ever saw and who raised me to appreciate the wonders of the White Rose, who were tireless in their provision of interesting details and wonderful dinners, and who I've spotted exchanging looks of amusement as my knowledge and enthusiasm grows. Thank must go to Malcolm Croft at Portico Books, whose elegant southern manners don't get in the way of his wisdom when it comes to deadlines, as well as the rest of the excellent Portico team, in particular Katie Cowan and designer Claire Marshall, for all their hard work.

Finally, a massive thank you to my very dear friend Steve Cann, who I dare say after thirty years in God's Own County has *almost* become a Yorkshireman.

JURASSIC YORKSHIRE
200,000,000 BC

Dinosaurs of old, and some surprisingly recent ones, have their feet firmly planted in Yorkshire. The eastern seaboard of the county, punctuated by its bonny collection of fishing villages tucked into the folds of cliffs, provides ample entertainment for the more nostalgic tourist, while harbouring Yorkshire's very own Jurassic Coast. If dinky fishing nets and rock pools are your thing, stranded starfish and crouching crabs are there to be found in abundance in Robin Hood's Bay and the beautiful Staithes. But as this coastline is battered for 90 per cent of the time by bracing winds and stormy seas, its erosion throws up constant supplies of ammonite and belemnite fossils to load the pockets of your best summer overcoat, anywhere you choose to wander between Scarborough and Cloughton.

The climate is not what it used to be. Two hundred million years ago it was balmy, subtropical even, and dinosaurs frolicked here on the beaches and wallowed in the shallow seas, which then covered most of Europe. Ichthyosaurus slipped dolphin-like through these waters, along with other marine reptiles such as teleosaurus and plesiosaur, and large grazing sauropods munched their way along the shores, keeping one eye out for more ominous carnivores. They were preserved where they fell, in mudstone and limestone, and now grace the walls of the wonderful Whitby Museum, a lost-attic-style treasure trove cluttered with interesting things, which visitors are actually encouraged to rummage through. Far more excitingly, there are real dinosaur footprints scattered along the coastline, evidence of three- and four-toed giants, which in some places appear to have splodged their way across the mudflats that very morning. You can literally follow in the footsteps of these great creatures, and feel connected to a time when dinosaurs walked the Earth. Because of the wear and tear of the weather, they don't always last, once exposed, and if you're really lucky, you could be the first to find footprints that have only recently been revealed.

It's not quite *Jurassic Park*, the 1993 Spielberg blockbuster with its hugely seductive 'meet the big guys' concept, which became the highest-grossing film ever on its release, but Yorkshire has its own connection with the movie. Set on a fictional island in the Pacific, where a team of genetic experts are paid to clone dinosaurs by a somewhat deluded billionaire with a helluva plan for a theme park, the movie was a milestone in the development of computer-generated imagery. Scenes where visitors experience real, living dinosaurs at close quarters are spectacularly evocative, thanks in part to a company of latex specialists at Aquaspersions in Charlestown, near Hebden Bridge, West Yorkshire. The team, which has provided materials for such classics as *The Muppets* and *Spitting Image* puppets, devised a special latex foam for production of the dinosaurs, and children of the upper Calder Valley remember their own moment of awestruck proximity to dinosaurs, when they watched the monstrous feet of Tyrannosaurus rex being loaded onto a flatbed trailer in preparation for their journey overseas to stardom.

BRITAIN'S OLDEST HOUSE

8770 BC

The history of the North is punctuated by buildings: Medieval York with its Roman and Viking edifices; castles like Skipton that bear the scars of sieges; and buildings from calmer times when wealth was not wasted on armies but used in the creation of spectacular country houses such as Castle Howard, whose lavish Baroque architecture became as familiar to the world as the teddy bear Aloysius in the TV dramatisation of *Brideshead Revisited*. There are the abbeys of Rievaulx, Jervaulx and Bolton, set in the magnificent rural splendour chosen by monks as wilderness retreats, the Minsters of York and Beverley, and of course there are the great mills of the Industrial Revolution. Tourists swarm the county in the summer, seeking accommodation in listed buildings with mullioned windows, happily banging their heads on low ceiling beams and losing their footing on clog-worn stone steps.

It should come as no surprise, then, that Britain's oldest house was found in Yorkshire, but not in the kind of condition that would offer even the most enthusiastic tourist an opportunity for a bump on the head. It lies, flatter than a wet pancake, under a peat bog in a field, but it is there all the same, and as it was built 11,000 years ago, it is very, very old.

Star Carr site on the east coast was first discovered in 1947 by amateur archaeologist John Moore, whose keen eye spotted an unusual number of flints turned up in freshly dredged drainage ditches. This find prompted an excavation by Professor Grahame Clark of Cambridge University and although later digs have disproved many of his theories, his is still one of the most important archaeological excavations ever in the study of British prehistory. Professor Clark found wood and bone items when all that usually remains of Mesolithic life are stone weapons and tools. There were around 200 projectile or harpoon points made of deer antler, elk, aurochs and bird bone, along with still rarer objects made from amber and shale. Twenty-one extraordinary stag antler skullcaps were unearthed, neatly bored with eye-holes, with the horns trimmed down and their insides smoothed for ease of wearing, but wearing for what? Hunting decoys or disguises, perhaps? Ritual headdresses maybe? It is hard to say, although later excavations suggest the latter is more probable. Europe's oldest example of carpentry was discovered in the form of a wooden platform made from split aspen and willow timbers on what was originally a lake shore, and Clark suspected from the number of animal remains around it that people had lived on it. More questions are being raised as others are answered, and the recent teams who have dug there say Star Carr is as important to an understanding of the Mesolithic period as Stonehenge is to the later Neolithic.

In the late 1980s further exploration of the site by Tim Schadla-Hall and Paul Lane developed a clearer picture of the landscape. Star Carr owes the survival of its relics to geographical events in the area. At the time it was inhabited, the ice age had ended and temperatures were similar to those today. However, the waters had not yet risen and Britain and the main continent of Europe were still connected. Star Carr, now about five miles from the seaside town of Scarborough, was originally on the banks of a lake known as Flixton, which over time was filled in by peat. Waterlogged peat (well known as a preserver of countless single welly boots claimed by suction from victims traversing moorland on such routes as the Pennine Way) has rare properties for protecting its contents for hundreds and thousands of years.

The most recent exploration in the 2000s, led by Nicky Milner, Chantal Collonner and Barry Taylor, sought to elaborate on the earliest dig by moving from the former lakeside up the nearby slopes. Eminent experts with fascinating job titles flocked to the site for samples of pre-historic flora and fauna and the team found that Europe's earliest example of carpentry was connected to a building. Castle Howard it was not: a 3.5m-wide structure made of poles and covered either with hide, thatch or turf, with a moss floor adjoining the platform which went out over the lake. It is not known how far the platform extended, nor exactly what it and the building were used for. The most recent theory is that the antler skullcaps were taken to the water's edge and placed there ceremoniously, perhaps in honour of the deer so essential to survival, a reverent gesture of thanks like a good old harvest festival. I've seen the prehistoric elk with its titanic antlers in the Leeds City Museum collection and it brings a whole new meaning to singing 'All Creatures Great and Small'.

The last excavation showed that the peat is beginning to recede and dry out in this area, making it a matter of urgency to fully explore the secrets of Star Carr before it's too late. This site was occupied for around 350 years, and there is more to discover. Given the prevalence these days of large groups of costumed merrymakers lurching from pub to pub in nearby seaside resorts, perhaps it is actually the site of Britain's oldest stag party!

THE STONEHENGE OF THE NORTH

3500–2500 BC

Thornborough Henges in North Yorkshire constitute one of the most important sites of ancient druidical rituals – whatever it was that druids did. These stunning constructions are the stuff of mystery and yet recent research has raised suggestions that they share a curious link with other ancient monuments around the world, from the Pyramids of Giza to the temples of the Aztecs in Latin America.

The Thornborough site consists of three neolithic henges, on a flat plateau between the rivers Ure and Swale. The henges, stone rings over 240 metres in diameter, are 550 metres apart and surrounded by a cursus, or platform of banks and ditches, which covers more than a mile of ground. The henges are laid out on a northwest-southeast alignment and are best viewed aerially because of their size. There is a peculiar dogleg angle to the three immaculate circles that simply does not look like an accident – in fact it looks strangely familiar. Archaeologists suggest the henges were designed specifically to mirror the three stars in the constellation of Orion's Belt, that most familiar group of stars, one of the easiest to recognise, and one that even very young children can pick out in the night sky. Many sophisticated computer programs and research grants later, it was ascertained that whoever built the henges between four and five thousand years ago aligned them so that the western end points towards the midwinter setting of Orion and the eastern end is aligned to its position at the midsummer solstice. The three henges have pairs of entrances, all of which share an axis in line with the sunrise at midwinter solstice, and which frame the ascent of Sirius, the brightest star, and one closely linked to Orion. Some of the banks have been destroyed by local quarrying, but when they were there, lined with gypsum to make them shimmer, they would have hidden the surrounding landscape from the people congregated inside the henges, giving them nothing but the night sky above upon which to focus. In the days before the yellowy sickness of light pollution tinged the skies and paled the stars, it would have felt as though they were practically in the heavens. It must have been intense and dramatic; a very old form of Sky TV!

Orion was first written about by the ancient Egyptians, and Christians suggested that the three stars were the wise men following Sirius to the nativity. In Australian aboriginal astronomy, Orion's Belt represents three brothers in a canoe. It has significance in all sorts of ancient cultures, from the Namoratunga of sub-Saharan Africa to the Bighorn Medicine Wheel in the mountains of Wyoming. It is possible that Orion, who is a hunter in mythology, became so significant because of his correlation with the movement of the midwinter sun. It is low in the winter, and Orion sets and rises in the same place, so it is possible that he was seen as pursuing the dying sun, with his disappearance, at the coming of spring, marking the return of light and warmth. The ancient Egyptians certainly associated the disappearance of Sirius and Orion for 70 days with death, matching the length of the mummification process specifically to it. The author Graham Hancock came up with the theory that the three Pyramids of Giza, like Thornborough Henge, are a mirror of Orion, and although some astronomers doubt his theory, he further points out that the Pyramid of the Sun at Teotihuacan in Mexico mirrors it likewise.

In the days before air travel, telescopes or computers, our ancient forebears could all have been connected through eyes on the skies. Who knows? As it says in the Book of Job, 'Canst thou bind the sweet influences of Pleiades, or loose the bands of Orion?'

A VERY OLD GENTLEMAN FROM GRISTHORPE

2035 BC

He was an old man of 60 when he died, and he had had a good life. Born into a wealthy family, he was well nourished in childhood, with a diet that included fish, meat and lots of fruit and vegetables. He was tall for his time at over six feet, athletic in build with a right arm as muscled as that of a world-class tennis player. As a young man of high status, he had been a warrior and had sustained many injuries – rib fractures, a broken jaw that had left his front teeth loose – but he was a good healer. Like many of us, he suffered a bad back in later life, having exerted himself strenuously while still growing, and the cyst that developed in his palate and expanded very slowly upwards towards his eye socket caused him splitting headaches and meant that he had to eat gingerly on one side to avoid the pain of it. His teeth were not in the best condition anyway, having been spoiled by too much honey. Eventually, a tumour in his brain got so big that he suffered fits and spells of weakness, auguring his end. Preparations were made for a ceremonial inhumation prior to his death: a turf barrow set into the hillside, a cairn of stones and a grand coffin fashioned from a whole oak trunk, hewn into the shape of hunched shoulders so that this noble man could crouch in the afterlife rather than take it lying down. He was buried in a cloak of hide, held with a pig-bone pin, and alongside him was a basket of food, his trusty whalebone-handled dagger made from Irish ore recycled several times, and a flint knife used since its first sharpening to cut meat and to scrape animal hides, which had been re-sharpened but not used since.

Gristhorpe Man was discovered in 1834 by William Beswick, a local landowner, near Filey, North Yorkshire, as he explored the largest of three turf barrows on what is now the Blue Dolphin Holiday Park caravan site. The art of conservation of ancient relics was far from perfect at that time, and the body was set to simmer for several hours in a laundry copper full of horse glue to keep it 'safe' from deterioration, a process which destroyed all future opportunities for analysis of collagen cells and suchlike. The discovery of this chieftain came ten years before the concept of the Three Age system, which was to establish a differentiation between the Stone, Bronze and Iron Ages. Nevertheless, William Crawford Williamson, the sparky 17-year-old son of the curator at Scarborough's Rotunda Museum, where Gristhorpe Man made his home after the grizzly glue-boiling experience, produced a tolerable report on the find, which he amended and updated over the years as more was learned, establishing the body as that of a Bronze Age lord.

In recent years, the Rotunda underwent refurbishment and Mr Gristhorpe was moved to Bradford University, where more sophisticated analysis went on. He even went to Bradford Royal Infirmary for a CT scan! Forensic facial reconstruction techniques have helped to recreate his features, and despite 60 years of battling with enemies and the bitter east coast climate, dying four thousand years ago, being boiled in glue, then spending another couple of hundred years wired together on display in Scarborough, we now know much detail about his life, and can even watch him speak on a computer screen.

A PERFECTLY PICKLED PREHISTORIC BRAIN
500 BC

The ancient Egyptians didn't think much of the brain as an organ. They extracted them through the nasal cavities of their deceased nobles with hooks, and threw them away, believing that the heart, lungs and other organs were of greater spiritual importance. In much later years, though, the preservation of significant brains became fashionable. Lenin's is still lovingly protected in wafer-thin slices (31,000 of them) behind layers of locked doors at the somewhat functionally named Moscow Brain Institute. Einstein's was removed on his death at the Princeton Hospital by a pathologist who divided it into 240 chunks, keeping much of it himself and distributing sections to friends and colleagues. He was fired when he refused to give it back. However, these and the noggin contents of other famous thinkers are mere spring chickens compared to the recent discovery of Iron Age grey matter in a particularly soggy bit of Yorkshire.

Scientists (and alliteration enthusiasts) were ecstatic when a bog in Heslington delivered up a rare treat in 2008: a perfectly preserved, prehistoric, pickled brain. The site where it was discovered, in the north of the county, is one that appears to have been used for ceremonial events up until Roman times and dating back as far as the Bronze Age. There are numerous pits, each originally marked with a single upright stake, and if the recent find is anything to go by, the ceremonies were far from picnics.

The brain was found inside a severed skull. The man it belonged to died in his thirties. Trauma to the vertebrae shows that he was executed by hanging and that immediately afterwards he was carefully decapitated with a sharp knife. The poor fellow's head was then consigned to the pit in which it lay for more than 2,000 years. The body of the man has not been found, although a headless red deer was discovered nearby. No one seems to suspect that this constitutes the ritual killing of some mythical sphinx-beast with the head of a man and the body of a deer, however. What remains is exciting enough, one of the world's best-preserved brains, described by investigators as being of a tofu-like consistency.

Brain tissue generally decomposes very quickly, but in the case of this one – the oldest intact brain found anywhere in Europe or Asia – it seems to have been preserved from harm by instant submersion, which prevented oxidisation. If the head had not been severed, the bacteria from intestine contents would have speeded the rotting process of the delicate grey matter (bodies have a tendency to eat themselves as the stomach bacteria remain hungry after death). It is still a mystery how the brain came to be so beautifully preserved though, as there was no evidence of embalming or smoking to help it along. Scientists have buried pig heads around the area in the hope that this might give some clues as to the special properties of this boggy land.

As an illustration of the diversity of research in this field, top neuroscientists are currently working on the cryopreservation of minute fragments of mammalian brains, believing that the storage of an organism's memories and personality in this way is just around the corner. They suggest that by the end of this century it will be possible to read stored brains like computer hard drives, accessing the memories of long-lost relatives and historical figures. If this were possible with our pickled friend, his last memory would certainly not upload as a happy one.

ST HILDA OF WHITBY AND CAEDMON THE COWHERD

614

St Hilda was my kind of saint. She was energetic, motherly, highly organised and a believer in comprehensive education, to the extent that she discovered the first English poet in a cowshed. She is said to have cured the region of a plague of snakes by turning them to stone, an explanation of the many ammonite fossils visible in the stones along the Whitby coast, some of which had snake heads carved onto them to 'prove it'. It is said that when gulls fly over Whitby Abbey, they dip their wings to salute Hilda, a woman of grace and understanding, who everyone called Mother.

Just about everything that is known of her comes from the Venerable Bede's *Ecclesiastical History of the English*, written around 731. His life overlapped that of the great St Hilda by about eight years. Hilda, or 'Hild' as she would have been known in her time, was one of the last Celtic princesses, the grandniece of King Edwin of Northumbria. Her father, Hereric, was in exile in the Celtic Kingdom of Elmet (now West Yorkshire) when he was murdered, leaving Hilda to be raised at King Edwin's court. Edwin was influenced by his wife, a Christian princess from Kent, and in a fit of religious enthusiasm had his entire court, including the teenaged Hilda, baptised into the faith on Easter Day, in a rickety wooden church knocked together for the occasion. The church, near the site of the future York Minster, may have fallen down in the next gust of wind, but the baptisms, performed by none other than the Bishop Paulinus, who had come from Rome with Augustine, held firm. Hilda was to become the founding abbess of a monastery in Streonshalh (Whitby); this was not any old abbey either, it was to be a great seat of learning, churning out bishops and well-educated clergymen. Hilda hosted the first ever English Christian synod, which debated such weighty topics as how to calculate the date of Easter, in an effort to unite customs shared by Roman and Celtic Christians so that people in the same area would celebrate on the same day. Although Hilda, who was raised a Celt, preferred their customs, she used her influence to encourage a peaceful acceptance of the synod's decision to calculate henceforward in the Roman way.

Hilda was a great teacher and administrator. She ran her monastery as a double house – men on one side, women on the other, with a chastening chapel in between – and it was very successful. Kings and high-ranking personages turned up from all over Europe seeking her wisdom and guidance, and yet she made herself available to the common man as well. In this way, the lowly, uneducated Caedmon became the author of the first recorded English poem.

Caedmon's role at the abbey was a smelly one: he tended the cows and herded them to pasture. He wasn't regarded as the life and soul of the party, being shy and ineloquent, and when his turn came to sing something at a feast he stumbled out into the night, embarrassed. No jelly and ice cream for Caedmon, it would seem, but a dream the same night is said to have inspired him to create verses praising Creation. He sought an audience with Hilda, who, with her egalitarian spirit, granted the request and as a consequence encouraged Caedmon to give up cows and focus on his literary pursuits.

St Hilda, as she became after her passing, became a symbolic figure for education. There are many colleges and seats of learning named after her, including St Hilda's College, Oxford, and that of St Hild and St Bede in Durham.

A MONSTROUS POGROM
1190

Saturday, 16 March 1190, a special Sabbath celebration relating to Passover, was marked by the horrific destruction of York's entire Jewish population. This was not the only attack on the Jewish communities of England around that time, but it was particularly gruesome and all-encompassing, and it left a lasting stain on York's reputation. A *Cherem*, a sort of religious taboo or curse, was said to have been laid on York, decreeing that Jews may not eat or spend the night in the city.

It was all down to money. The church forbade Christians from lending money in the twelfth century, and Jews were forbidden from engaging in most regular occupations with the exclusion of charging interest on loans, so it's hardly surprising that they became money-lenders. Henry II gave his protection to the Jews because the Crown received hefty dividends from these financiers; still, the Jews became affluent and the English people resented them, in spite of the many restrictions laid upon them and the three-times higher taxes they paid.

When Richard I took over the long-coveted throne of his father in 1189, a deputation of leading Jews brought lavish gifts to Westminster Abbey for the new king. Superstition prevented the guards from admitting them to the coronation hall and the assembled crowds outside took this humiliation as a welcome sign of the new king's rejection of the old king's protected subjects. Trouble broke out. When Richard heard of this, he sent out a proclamation to all his realms to dispel the rumour, but with one foot on the ship ready to embark on a Holy Crusade, he was not going to be around to enforce it. The Crusading spirit of the age fuelled all sorts of hatred against Muslims and Jews alike, adding to the general resentment of the Jews in Europe at that time.

In 1190, a mob attacked the Jews of the city of York, beginning with the palatial house of Baruch, a leading Jew who was one of those refused entry to the coronation. The mob, incited by Richard Malebisse, burned the thatch from Jewish houses and looted wealth. The terrified families sought refuge in the royal castle, claiming their right to the King's protection. The castle warden went in search of the sheriff but on his return, the Jews were so afraid of the wild rabble that was escalating by the minute outside, they feared he would betray them and refused to let him back in. The castle was surrounded, the crowds were baying for Jewish blood, and for two days a monk preached destruction, inciting the crowd to murder. The sheriff then ordered the castle to be reclaimed by force, something the mob were itching to do, and when a falling stone from the roof took out the monk mid-sentence, they became wild with rage and attacked.

A terrible choice faced the 150 Jews inside the keep. They could capitulate and be baptised, while still risking being torn to pieces by the mob outside, they could stay and be burned with the wooden keep, or they could take their own lives. Leading Rabbi Yomtob of Joigny proposed taking their own lives, as a more dignified option to handing themselves over to the murderous rabble raging outside. Almost the entire York Jewish community died violently that night. Most committed suicide, the men dispatching their women and children before taking their own lives, while others were consumed in the flames which left the keep a charred ruin. The remainder, who pleaded for mercy, were murdered by the crowd. Malebisse and his cronies burned all the documents relating to their debts before fleeing to Scotland, thus eradicating the large sums of money owed to the Jews, and therefore also to the Crown.

The brutal destruction of this community did not go wholly unpunished. Many in the city were fined and Richard I amended the law so that double records were to be kept henceforth to protect money owed to the Crown. The main perpetrators had all escaped, however, and were never brought to task.

The Cherem curse is said to relate back to this date, although by the beginning of the thirteenth century, the Jewish community had largely re-established itself in York. Still, persecution of Jewish communities began to rise again in England, and worse was to come in 1290 when Edward I seized all Jewish property, expelled the entire population of Jewish subjects and made all outstanding debts they were owed payable to the Crown. Jews were not readmitted to England until 1656.

There is no evidence that the Cherem was ever officially invoked, however at a ceremony at the site in 1978, the then Chief Rabbi Lord Jakobovits lifted it along with the Archbishop of York, Dr Stuart Blanch. Today there are only a very few Jews living in York, and Clifford's Tower, built on the site of the charred keep, stands as a warning to us to learn from history's mistakes and defend against prejudice and racism.

On Holocaust Memorial Day, 27 January, the anniversary of the liberation of Auschwitz concentration camp by the Russians in 1945, members of the Jewish faith lay pebbles at the foot of Clifford's Tower. This custom of Pesikta Zutra remembers the dead and says, 'I am here, I have not forgotten.'

ROBIN HOOD – LIVED AT ONE SERVICE STATION, DIED AT ANOTHER

CIRCA 1200

The story of Robin Hood has flourished since its advent, although there is no way yet found to calculate exactly when that was. It has been told, embellished and retold for the past 800 years and is known throughout the world. Just about anyone can name one or more of his Merry Men, his girlfriend, his adversaries, his motivations, where he lived, how he lived, how he died, and still the enigma of Robin Hood has been a challenge for scholars almost since the legend began. Whether he actually existed at all is less than conclusive. However, it seems almost certain that the bowman in Lincoln Green whose image graces the road signage on entering and exiting Nottinghamshire, the outlaw whose famed haunt was Sherwood Forest, was actually a Yorkshireman. Well, of course!

Robin Hood may be no more real than his modern incarnation as principal boy in tights and tunic, exchanging thigh-slapping banter with the pantomime dame. This is quite fitting given that most 'evidence' of his existence comes from five old ballads of the 'Robin Hode in Scherewode stode' variety, and as that is what we have to rely on for much historical information, so be it.

The earliest surviving literary reference is in William Langland's poem 'Piers Plowman', written around 1377. A character named Sloth confesses that he doesn't know the Lord's Prayer perfectly, but he can recite rhymes of Robin Hood from memory. That oral tradition of poems no longer exists but this reference shows us that one hundred or so years after his time, Robin Hood had already 'gone viral'.

Exhaustive scholarly exploration has uncovered records of villains up and down the country whose crimes and attendant fines had been logged under the surname Robehod or Rabunhod between 1261 and 1296. It is unclear whether this criminal nickname was assumed by the lawbreakers themselves or given to them as a form of categorisation, but it shows that in the mid- to late thirteenth century, Robin Hood, the legendary outlaw, was also nationally acknowledged in official records.

By the 1490s, tales of Robin began to appear in some of the earliest print. A long poem entitled 'A Gest of Robyn Hode' made it into at least five different editions, one of which still exists in its entirety and was published by the evocatively named Wynken de Worde, a much-renowned English printer of the time. De Worde was a typographer and in 1500 became the first to set up a print house in Fleet Street, beginning the trend which would make this quarter of London synonymous with printing for centuries to come. He cannot, however, be held responsible for Rupert Murdoch.

The Gest (meaning history) was probably written around 1400, but the author is unknown. It consists of 456 four-line stanzas, beginning in the greenwood at Barnsdale with Robin and his men preparing to feast and ending, after various adventures, with the betrayal and death of the hero. Many features of the legend's future developments can be found in the Gest. Robin will not declare the feast open until a guest is brought and sends Will Scarlock, Little John and Much the Miller's son to find one. They return with a knight, poorly clad, who has been tricked out of his estate by the mean old abbot of St Mary's in York. Robin Hood, on hearing his tale, decides to help. The abbot is outwitted, the knight reinstated to his lands and his money returned twofold.

The roots of robbing the rich to give to the poor are discernible here and also in Robin's general approach to travellers waylaid as they pass through the greenwood. He asks them what they have, then has them searched. If they have spoken the truth about their possessions they get to keep them; if they have lied, they don't. It is easy to see that those with very little, or nothing at all, would probably be more honest than an abbot with full coffers to conceal, but there is also the implication that the honourable conduct of the poor knight deserves fair treatment and assistance while the arrogance and surliness of the abbot justifies exploitation.

Like all the best superheroes, Robin Hood has arch-enemies who occasionally surface while he continues his fight against evil untouched by time or political change. He has no long-term plan, he just reacts to whatever comes through his woodland home. Robin is an outlaw with a code of ethics and a cheeky talent for cocking a snook at authority, an outlook that has drawn him a devoted audience throughout history. Is it that 'outlaw with a heart of gold' trait which makes his legend so incredibly enduring? The answer is as elusive as the man himself, but Robin Hood has not only endured, his legend constantly grows and changes with each new medium for storytelling, from minstrel songs and plays, to print and on to films incorporating the latest special effects. His well-travelled name has even been applied to the international Robin Hood Tax campaign, a massive initiative promoted by non-governmental organisations including Christian Aid, Comic Relief and Unicef, which calls for a social welfare tax on stocks and shares transactions. Surely our hero would have been impressed.

There is no Maid Marion in the Gest, she has not yet been written into the legend and Robin is motivated by a pious devotion to the Virgin Mary rather than his later-attributed earthly love. Towards the middle of the Gest, Little John takes part in an archery contest presided over by the Sheriff of Nottingham and the adventures move to the locale of Sherwood.

'Robin Hoode His Death', a 27-verse fragment, appears to relate to the Gest and also deals with Robin's betrayal by his cousin, the Prioress of Kirklees, whom he visits for medical treatment. It is eventually discovered that she has a secret lover, Sir Roger of Doncaster, and she is over-bleeding Robin, ostensibly for his health, as part of a plot to kill him. Robin slays Sir Roger, forgives the Prioress as he loves God and asks Little John to lay him in his grave. 'And set my bright sword at my head / My arrows at my feet / And lay my yew-bow by my side ...' Lovely words.

Although the famous shooting of his last arrow to mark the place for his burial is not in the Gest or in what remains of 'His Death', the location is consistent in all re-tellings: Kirklees Priory at Hartshead, near Huddersfield. The tale begins at Barnsdale near Doncaster and only moves intermittently in action to Nottinghamshire. J.C. Holt, a

Bradford-born academic, Professor Emeritus of Medieval History at the University of Cambridge and a meticulous scholar who is generally hailed as the last word on Robin Hood, has shown that the likeliest candidate for the man himself appears in the York assizes of 1225: Robert Hod, the outlaw. He is there again the following year in the Yorkshire Pipe Roll with the added nickname 'Hobbehod', which may be indicative of the legend's emerging.

According to these earliest known sources, it is most likely that if he existed at all, Robin Hood was born at Barnsdale, South Yorkshire – site of Barnsdale Bar Services on the A1 where travellers brace themselves to this day, not to face philanthropic wealth-redistribution specialists, but to pay a king's ransom for a Full English and the use of a leaky teapot. Robin's end came about at Kirklees Priory next to Hartshead Moor Services on the M62 between Leeds and Huddersfield, where the breakfast is about the same as at Barnsdale, but the views are a little better.

TOLLING THE DEVIL'S KNELL
1434

It's Christmas Eve in Dewsbury, a minster town in West Yorkshire, and some very burly bell-ringers are flexing their muscles for the annual local marathon to ward off evil. Black Tom, the Devil's Bell at Dewsbury Minster Church of All Saints', is tolled once for each year since Christendom began with the birth of Jesus and is no small undertaking in 2012. By midnight their work will be done and the first Eucharist of Christ-Mass will declare the devil defeated. That's the general idea, anyway.

The tradition began in 1434 when a devout but hot-tempered local knight, Sir Thomas de Soothill, noticed that one of his servant boys had failed to attend the Sunday service. He confronted the boy and, in a raging fit of fury, raised him above his head and threw him into the millpond. The boy couldn't swim and was drowned in calm depths of cold water. De Soothill's anger subsided into remorse as he realised what he had done and for what purpose. He had certainly secured the boy's attendance in church!

In an act of penance the knight commissioned a new bell for the parish, a 1300lb tenor bell, with the wish that it should be tolled at his own funeral and that members of the community should pray for his immortal soul. 'Black Tom' (named after de Soothill) was to be rung for each year of Our Lord before the Yuletide Midnight Mass to celebrate each year of grace, and to proclaim the death of the devil and forgiveness of all sins. A life sentence for murder might have been more appropriate, but de Soothill sidestepped that one nicely, distracting attention from his own crime and focusing it on a much greater villain. Some say that it is a knell for Lucifer being killed by the Nativity and call the ceremony 'Old Lad's Passing', although the more common Christian belief that the incarnation of God in human form marked the beginning of the end for the Evil One interprets the ringing of Black Tom more as a means of taunting the Devil.

Unlike many of these strange ancient rituals, tolling the Devil's Knell in Dewsbury has retained a certain sombre authenticity. Aside from appearing on a Royal Mail commemorative stamp as part of the 1980s 'Traditions of England' series, it has not become a media-fuelled tourist attraction embellished with burger stands and funfairs, as have so many local customs. There are no attendant rituals at all, just the usual minster bell-ringers and a tally keeper to keep the count from about 10.15, when the monotonous tolling begins.

Its effectiveness may be in question, as Dewsbury remains a rather troubled town. It went through a period of serious decline after its successful mill industry began to crumble in the wool crisis of 1950. Dewsbury contains some of the poorest communities in Britain, causing a divide between indigenous and immigrant populations, but was not without its share of turbulence long before that. It was a centre for Luddite activity, when the retaliation of workers against mechanisation of the mills became a bitter fight in the early nineteenth century. This began its own rather odd tradition, that of a gun being fired at ten o' clock each night to signal all was calm. The 'Ten O Clock' continued until recently, except in wartime, and could be heard all over the area. A funny way to signal a peaceful evening if ever there was one.

Dewsbury was also the scene of Chartist agitation when a 7,000-strong crowd laid siege to the Poor Law Guardians in the town centre in 1838. Again in 1840, agitators demanding reform seized control of the town and troops had to be called in to disperse the protest.

In recent years, a series of high-profile crime reports led to media references to poor old Dewsbury as 'the town that dare not speak its name'. The Yorkshire Ripper, Peter Sutcliffe, was arrested in 1981 and questioned at Dewsbury police station. In 2005 two shocking events occurred in the same month which put the town under a harsh media spotlight. Mohammad Sidique Khan, a Dewsbury man, part of the quartet who came to be known as the 7/7 Bombers, detonated a device on London Underground's Circle Line, killing himself and seven other people. Meanwhile, back home in Yorkshire, a twelve-year-old girl was found guilty of grievous bodily harm after she attempted to hang a five-year-old boy, who she strung up from a tree and beat with sticks and nettles, binding his throat and genitals and bringing him within inches of losing his life.

The town's image was further tarnished by the massive media and police campaign to find nine-year-old Shannon Matthews, who went missing from Dewsbury Moor in 2008. Amid tremendous community support, Shannon's mother and her boyfriend appealed for news of the little girl, who was found several weeks later under the bed of the boyfriend's uncle. He was arrested and Shannon's family enjoyed a champagne-fuelled street party, courtesy of neighbours, while the uncle slit his wrists in custody and police investigations turned up child-porn images on the boyfriend's computer, before discovering the mother's involvement in the abduction of her own daughter. Dewsbury became infamous and the town's many hard-working, decent people going on holiday found themselves hesitating when asked by other holidaymakers where they were from, choosing to say 'Yorkshire' rather than their more accurate geographical location. Such is the influence of the media.

Still, Sir Thomas de Soothill wanted his death knell ringing not just to defy evil but for the sins of all. The poet John Donne cautioned against people asking for whom the bell tolls in his famous poem of 1624, saying 'no man is an island entire and of itself. Each is a continent, a part of the main.' We are all responsible in some way as members of mankind, he suggested, by which reckoning, the Devil's Bells in Dewsbury don't just toll for the Devil and they don't just toll for some short-fused old lord who killed his servants willy-nilly for bunking off church; they toll for the nicking of a Mars bar from the village shop, for pulling a sickie at work, or being snappy with the children because you are in a rush; they toll for mass-murderers, child abductors and radical agitators; they toll for me and they toll for thee, 2,012 times and counting …

A MAN OF 'ROMAN RESOLUTION'
1570

On 13 April 1570, a son was born into a church-going Protestant family on Stonegate in York. As his parents gazed down at the newly arrived, bouncing baby boy, I bet neither of them thought to themselves what a shame it would be if he became a fundamentalist Catholic terrorist, tried to blow the King and his government into smithereens, and ended up as Britain's number one bogeyman, effigy of choice for the annual ritual burnings of half a millennium to come.

Guy Fawkes is a household name associated with fire, fun and food. His father died when he was just eight years old and his mother remarried, to a Catholic. Thus, the young Guy was converted, and his embrace of Catholicism became the defining feature of his life. He sold his father's estate when he came of age, and set off to fight on the side of Catholic Spain in the Eighty Years' War against the Dutch Protestants. He was a good soldier, recommended for a captaincy, and his enthusiasm for the cause led him to visit King Philip of Spain to ask for support in stirring up a rebellion against James I, back home in Blighty. Spain was technically at war with England at this time, but Philip wasn't interested in the idea so Guy, who had by this time adopted the more Latin version of his name and answered to Guido, set off for Flanders, where he got involved with some like-minded individuals who were hatching a scheme to blow up the King.

Guido was tall and strong, friendly and appealing, a keen debater, with a high threshold for pain and a low one for rude manners. His knowledge of explosives made him an important member of the Gunpowder Plot and it fell to him to source and handle the necessary incendiaries. This was no mean feat, and he and the gang, under the leadership of Robert Catesby, spent a year and a half preparing to blast the Houses of Parliament, along with the 'heretic' King, to kingdom come. They at first tried to tunnel their way under from nearby lodgings; easier said than done, as any child who has ever decided to spend their summer holidays digging a tunnel to Australia will corroborate. If they ever really got started on the tunnel, no evidence of it has ever been uncovered, but the gang found an alternative in renting a disused undercroft that reached under their target. The House's opening session was delayed in 1605, due to an outbreak of the plague, and as a result the first massive consignment of gunpowder Guido had managed to procure was stashed down there in the mouldy cellar for so long that it deteriorated beyond use. He had to set about replacing the 36 barrels with a fresh stock, which he concealed behind a fuel store of wood and coal.

As the day approached, one of the gang sent an anonymous letter to a Catholic Member of Parliament, Lord Monteagle, warning him to stay away from the proceedings. The letter was shown to the King, who prepared his men. Finally, on the evening of 4 November, the gang took their positions to wait for morning. Guido was the one who was to light the fuse and he sat in the cellar until late in the night with a slow-burning taper and a watch. He was discovered around midnight by the King's men. Talk your way out of that one, Guido!

To his credit, he didn't even try. When asked what he intended to do with 36 barrels of gunpowder, he is reported as replying that it was 'to blow you Scotch beggars back to your native mountains'. He did try to avoid giving up the names of his fellow conspirators, and underwent two days of torture before he cracked. King James praised him as a man of 'Roman resolution' for his dignity under torture, before sending him to face the worst possible penalty the realm could conceive. High treason was a crime which demanded more than a little slap on the wrist. He was to be hung, then cut down while still alive to witness his own tackle being chopped off and burned on a fire, then his innards were to be made into outards, followed up by the *coup de grâce* of being hacked into quarters to be sent to all points of the compass.

Two other plotters were executed at the same time, on 31 January 1606, while Robert Catesby was killed attempting to escape on the night the plot was uncovered; but it is Guy Fawkes who is remembered. Guido denied the crowd a significant part of the spectacle, and saved himself from a significant part of the suffering, by sidestepping the executioner and hurling himself from the scaffold just before the noose was put in place. He broke his neck in the fall. A mercy! Even those who think his crime was a terrible one find his confession signature upsetting. After the rack and all else they did to him, it is the shaky hand of a broken man who was signing his name for the last time.

Not everyone remembers Guy Fawkes with ill-feeling, in fact he is linked with one of the most traditional feasts in the English calendar, especially in his home county of Yorkshire, where there is a keenness to the pleasure of a boiling-hot front and a freezing-cold back on many a bonfire night. Some choose to vent more contemporary ire, making effigies of unpopular figures, such as Margaret Thatcher. Guido's school, St Peter's in York, the fourth oldest school in the world, which was opened by St Paulinus in 627, still opts out of the Guy Fawkes Night tradition in honour of their Old Peterite alumnus, and there are those who still raise a glass in cynical moments to 'the last man to enter Parliament with honest intentions'.

DICK TURPIN, SWIFT NICK NEVISON AND WHAT REALLY HAPPENED BETWEEN LONDON AND YORK

1676

In a dark, dank, icy cell in York Castle sat a man called John Palmer, who was really Dick Turpin, who wasn't really the great highwayman his name evokes. Confused? So were the authorities who held this man captive on a charge of horse rustling in January 1739. There were around 200 offences punishable by death in England at this time, and whoever he was, whatever the charge, he was soon to be dancing at the end of a short rope. How Turpin came to be identified and how he came to be such a famous 'Gentleman of the Highway' is a strange tale indeed.

Richard Turpin was a butcher's son, born in Essex. He followed the family trade, adding his own twist of lawlessness: he was part of a gang who poached the King's deer and jointed and dressed them for sale in the high street. Turpin was a sly, dishonourable rogue, unprepossessing, his face scarred by smallpox. He moved on from butchery to violent burglaries, first with the Essex gang and later with other accomplices. His crimes, which involved harsh treatment of his victims, soon earned him a price on his head. After several attacks on farmhouses, where maids were raped, faces slashed and family members stripped and held over the fire, bounty hunters soon put an end to most of the band. Turpin escaped, and adapted himself to highway robbery. With a price of £200 on his head (nearly £30,000 in modern terms), he thought nothing of popping off the occasional rustic swain who might identify him, and when things down South got a little too hot and his name became a little too well known, he moved to the northern capital, supplementing his income by stealing steeds in Lincolnshire and flogging them off above the Humber.

In York he assumed an alias and set about a seemingly respectable life, lodging at an inn and joining hunting parties with local gentlemen. Some were curious as to how he came by his income, suspecting him, quite rightly, of horse theft, and when he shot his landlord's cockerel one day in a fit of 'fowl' temper after a poor hunt, and then waved his gun in the faces of his companions, threatening to shoot them too, he was arrested pending investigation, bringing us back to the point where he sat in a York Castle cell under the name of John Palmer.

So long as no one learned who he was, Turpin was fairly confident of getting out of this scrape alive. Horse stealing was a capital offence, along with a couple of hundred or more other crimes in England's 'Bloody Code', the most comprehensive capital punishment list in Europe. Such irredeemable sins as spending a month in the company of gypsies could earn a death penalty, as could 'strong evidence of malice' in a child aged 7 to 14. Turpin needed a character reference from a respectable person in order to have a chance of being deported instead of being hanged. To this end he wrote a letter to his brother-in-law, Pompr Rivernall, in Hempstead. Rivernall took one look at the writing on the envelope and refused to pay the postage to collect it. He may well have been sick of his wife's embarrassing brother by this time and probably wanted to distance himself from Turpin's reputation, so the letter was returned to the postmaster's office in Saffron Walden in Essex. Strangely enough, the postmaster of Saffron Walden happened to be the very same man who had taught Dick Turpin to write, twenty-odd years previously at the village school. He recognised the hand, opened the letter, and set off to York to identify the prisoner and claim his reward.

Turpin was convicted under his real name for the crimes he had carried out as John Palmer to save the trouble of moving him south: theft of a mare worth three pounds, a foal worth twenty shillings and a gelding worth about the same as the mare. The people of York were impressed by the celebrity of the prisoner and the jailer is said to have made nearly a hundred pounds in selling liquor to visitors of the condemned man. A queue of women formed to 'pay their respects' – not very respectably, wishing to acquire carnal knowledge of the notorious highwayman. One way or another, Turpin was kept well entertained until his execution on 7 April 1739. He used the last of his ill-gotten gains to hire mourners to follow him a-weeping to the gallows and, due to his notoriety, to pay a guard to watch over his grave after the event. Bodysnatchers did indeed attempt to take his corpse from the freshly turned soil, but they were thwarted.

This would have been the end of his brief fame for an ignominious collection of shoddy crimes, had it not been for a couple of Williams: one born a hundred years before him and one a hundred years after his death. The latter, novelist William Harrison Ainsworth, immortalised Dick Turpin as the hero of his 1834 novel *Rookwood*, attributing all sorts of daring feats and suave encounters to the pox-ridden little scallywag. Turpin's fabled ride to York on bonny Black Bess, which caught the hearts and imaginations of six editions' worth of readers in English and several more in French and German when first published, was in reality accomplished by another highwayman, William 'Swift Nick' John Nevison. Dare I say it – a Yorkshireman!

Born in Wortley around 1639, the son of a respectable man of means, Nevison became a famous and flamboyant highwayman. He was altogether more in the hero mould and the account of his incredible ride to York had already been on record for some time, while Turpin was just a butcher's lad. The mare he rode was a bay, not black, and she wasn't called Bess, but on a summer's morning in 1676 Nevison had held up a traveller in Gad's Hill, Kent, and made his escape by crossing the Thames on a ferry and galloping his horse to Chelmsford, then Cambridge, then Huntingdon, and on up the Great North Road to York. This stunning journey was accomplished by sunset through skill and judgement in riding and through the stamina of the horse, which Nevison rested for regular but brief periods to sustain the journey. After a quick change of clothes and a short saunter to a bowling green where the Lord Mayor was wont to play, Nevison engaged this lofty personage in conversation and struck a bet over the game at eight o'clock. When he was later arrested for the Gad's Hill robbery, he produced the Lord Mayor as a witness, convincing the court that he could not have been responsible for a crime 200 miles away on the very same day. He was acquitted.

Unlike Turpin, Nevison was known for being a fine figure of a man and for his careful avoidance of harming those he robbed. He was also popular for the flourish and bravado with which he evaded the noose, even escaping gaol by posing as a plague victim and leaving in a coffin. This he accomplished by enlisting the help of a friend and physician to diagnose him as extremely infectious, and an artist to paint on the bluish bruise-like marks of the plague. Far more worthy of heroic stories, he was nevertheless rather a scoundrel, and after killing a constable who tried to arrest him, he too was eventually caught by bounty hunters and hanged at York Castle in 1684, about half a century before spotted Dick would follow him up the same steps.

AN UNEDUCATED YORKSHIRE LAD WHO GAVE US THE BRITISH EMPIRE

1693

On 24 March 1693 John Harrison was born in Foulby, near Wakefield. From a poor family, and with no education, he was one of those rare treasures of evolution, a lone genius. He devoted his life to solving a problem that such exalted scientists as Newton suspected was impossible: that of finding longitude at sea.

It wasn't plain sailing for Harrison, whose humble origins and miraculous feats of engineering combined to raise the hackles of the scientific establishment. Very little is known about his life or how he came to be such a master of clock-making, but the four portable precision timekeepers he designed are still alive and ticking, though the Empire they made possible has been and gone.

Latitude and longitude have chequered the planet since ancient times. The astronomer Ptolemy had laid them out on maps in the world's first atlas by AD 150. Latitude is fixed by nature as a zero-degree parallel at the Equator, where the heavenly bodies pass directly overhead, and is easy enough for any experienced sailor to gauge; longitude, on the other hand, has no fixed natural mark and is only measurable through a knowledge of the time it is back at your home port to compare to the relative position of the sun and stars wherever you are at sea. This doesn't seem like much of a problem now, when even a Christmas-cracker watch will keep its time upon the wave, however up until the end of the eighteenth century the lack of a clock capable of operating accurately during a sea voyage had dropped even the most talented sailors into the hands of fate. Sir Francis Drake, Christopher Columbus and all other captains in the Age of Exploration followed a line along the your-guess-is-as-good-as-mine latitude in a time where new continents suddenly appeared through the mist, or didn't, depending on the luck of the draw.

Ships were constantly crashing into land they'd guesstimated as being weeks away and losses were great. A particularly persistent fog in the autumn of 1707 caused Admiral Sir Clowdisley Shovell to pile the English fleet into the Scillies as they returned home victorious from clashes with the French near Gibraltar. Of the 2,000 men, only two made it to shore alive. This dreadful incident was yet another in the catalogue of seafaring disasters: tales of scurvy and shipwrecks litter maritime history and most relate to the inability to measure longitude on the pitch and toss of a deck. Something had to be done and the great naval nations all offered bounties to anyone who could come up with a practical answer to the problem. The British government offered the largest prize of all in its Longitude Act of 1714. The £20,000 purse, equivalent to several million pounds in current terms, was coveted by many a great scientist, although finding longitude at sea had become a sort of Holy Grail, unattainable and elusive in its legendary significance.

Needless to say, such a prize attracted all manner of quacks and bounty hunters into the fray, including one 'wounded dog' theory first put forward in 1687 and based on a cure called Powder of Sympathy. This quack compound, discovered by Sir Kenelm Digby on his travels through France, was said to have a unique remote healing capability. If applied to a possession of the ailing one, it could heal a wound at long distance. The process apparently involved some smarting and prompted the suggestion that taking a wounded dog to sea and having someone back in port apply Powder of Sympathy to one of its previously worn dressings at noon sharp every day would cause the hound to yelp. The time difference between noon at home, and noon on board – when the sun is at its highest point – would allow the sailor a fair stab at calculating his longitude, if he could concentrate with the dog yapping. The RSPCA was not to be founded until 1824, but in this case it was hardly needed to find fault with this enthusiastically far-out suggestion. The sheer daftness of it speaks for itself.

Far away from the royal observatories and astronomical societies of learned men, young John Harrison caught a whiff of the challenge.

He was a carpenter with no training in clock-making, firmly convinced that the answer to the problem lay in creating an accurate timepiece. As a teenager, Harrison had taught himself to read and write to do justice to a book lent to him by a visiting clergyman. He honed his skill by copying out and annotating the entire work: a series of lectures by a Cambridge mathematician, complete with diagrams. Writing it out word for word gave him an understanding of the laws of motion and he cleaved to this book like a bible for years.

Harrison's first clock was finished before he was 20. This unique timepiece, as might be expected of a carpenter, was entirely made out of wood. Historians remain baffled as to how Harrison could have found a clock to dismantle and study in order to make his own. Clocks were rare and expensive in the early eighteenth century and if his family had been able to afford one, they probably wouldn't have found anywhere to buy it. There simply was no known clockmaker within a hundred miles of the Harrisons' home. It is quite possible that it was this lack of any apprenticeship that provided Harrison with an unfettered mind for blue-sky thinking, as each new clock he fashioned contained innovation after revolutionary innovation. To counter the problem of lubricants deteriorating in changing climates at sea, he used lignum vitae, an oil-producing wood. He dealt with the troublesome expansion and contraction of pendulums by making them from grids of brass and iron designed to exactly compensate each other's alteration in varying atmospheres, so that the swing remained the same. In order to go after the prize, Harrison had to move on to working with metal, which he did, and the engineering innovations continued to flow. He even found a way to keep the pendulum upright, no matter how much the ship rolled.

Although this low-born ill-educated tradesman was regarded with suspicion by many in the establishment, he was supported by Astronomer Royal Edmund Halley (of comet fame) and watchmaker George Graham, who was so impressed with Harrison's staggering abilities that he lent him money on trust to further his research. Still, the Board of Longitude was against him as a champion of the chronographic approach, when the lofty minds of the time remained convinced that the answer lay in charting the moon. They continually moved the goalposts and indulged in all sorts of foul play to avoid awarding Harrison the longitude prize, even though his beautiful clocks stood up to the test of sea voyages with astonishing accuracy.

Harrison was in his eighties and rapidly becoming a bitter man by the time King George III intervened in 1772. He had an active interest in science and had followed the trials of Harrison's clocks; after an interview with John's son and partner, William, he is said to have declared, 'By God, Harrison, I will see you righted!' Whether or not he actually said these words, he certainly acted on them. He had his own private observatory oversee the trials of Harrison's H5 watch (the size had come down a bit over the years) and helped circumnavigate the Board of Longitude and its moon-prejudiced machinations by a direct appeal to Parliament for justice to be done to the Harrison achievement. In June 1773 it prevailed, and Harrison received close to the sum total of the prize money. Two years later, fellow Yorkshireman Captain Cook extolled the virtues of Harrison's achievement as he accurately charted the South Sea Islands. The ship's log of HMS *Resolution* has many references to 'our trusty friend the Watch' and 'our never failing guide'.

Men like John Harrison are a rare treat, calling for a big-up for the underdog (not the wounded one) who solved the greatest scientific problem of his time. His magnificent chronometers, which afforded the English such expanding prowess at sea, are now honoured as they should be, visited by thousands every year in the Maritime Museum at Greenwich, where each morning they are reverently unlocked and wound by white-gloved hands.

JOHN METCALF –
A TRUE YORKSHIRE FORCE
1717

John Metcalf was born in 1717 and lived until he was 93. A violinist, stagecoach driver, card player, cock fighter, hunter to hounds, a fish merchant, a horse dealer, a race winner, a soldier and a famously talented pioneer of road building, he would deserve a mention anyway for his industrious existence but, quite incredibly, Metcalf did all this and more in spite of being as blind as a stone from smallpox since the age of six.

Blind Jack of Knaresborough, as he came to be known, adapted himself to his affliction rapidly. Within six months of his illness he could navigate his way along Knaresborough's main street without assistance and within three years had a detailed grasp of the whole town. He was tutored in the violin as a boy because his parents were anxious he should find a way of making a living that might accommodate his disability. His father was a horse dealer, hardly a suitable trade to pass on to one's blind son, but Jack mastered riding as easily as the violin, maintaining a talent for horsey activities all his life. Growing up, he engaged in all the usual *Just William* pursuits of young village lads. No laden fruit tree was safe, whatever the wall around it. He was a keen bird nester and poacher and 'borrowed' couples of hounds from local huntsmen until he could procure his own in later years. He grew to be a tall, young man, a fine physical specimen, a jack-the-lad who caught the eye of local damsels and got more than one into trouble. At over six feet in height he was a strong swimmer and retrieved things from deep water that others could not: lost yarn, logs, even bodies. Did I mention he was blind?

In his youth, Jack earned a decent living playing his fiddle at country dances in the local area and at assemblies in Harrogate, where he had regular employment at the Queen's Head, the George and Dragon, and the Marquis of Granby Inn. Maybe just to show the sighted what he was capable of, he acted as a local guide to travellers, with the added advantage of providing an equal quality of service whether it was day or night. He once guided a gentleman from York to Harrogate in the dark, hoping he wouldn't be rumbled for his blindness and lose the job. It was 1735 and the turnpike road was years away from construction but Jack had learned his way through careful observation of the changes in terrain under his horse's shoes and such natural signposts as the sound of the wind in geographical landmarks. Jack was a dude, and one known by everyone in his area, so his cover on this journey was nearly blown a couple of times when friendly folk called out as he passed. Ironically, the generally poor visibility saved him from discovery when someone shouted, 'Eyup – it's Blind Jack!' Jack winced a little and kept quiet until the villager's companion told his friend he must be mistaken and our sightless hero avoided detection. After he had brought his gentleman safely to the Granby Inn he was invited in for a drink. It had been a long night and Jack was not quite on his usual form, going wide a couple of times when reaching for his ale. When he went to check on the horses the gentleman remarked to the landlord, Christopher Benson (who deserves to be named for his later connection to this tale), that his guide must have downed some spirits since they arrived. The landlord, cottoning on to the fact that the traveller had no idea his guide was blind, enlightened him. The stunned traveller called for Jack to be brought in, telling him he would never have engaged him if he'd known. Then, sensing the twinkle in Jack's useless eyes, he realised he had been safely deceived, paid Jack an extra two guineas, and treated him to food and drink throughout the whole of the following day.

It seems hard to believe at times just how much life this man lived. He was not even 21 years old by this point in his history and his resourcefulness knew no bounds. In 1737 he eloped with Dolly Benson, daughter of his landlord friend Christopher, on the eve of her officially intended marriage to a man of suitable standing. Aided in every intrigue by his friends – in this case an ostler who lent him his master's stout mare to carry off the maiden in the night and another to watch for Dolly's signal of a candle in her window – Jack Metcalf is a man-monument to the Yorkshire code of respect for those who don't whinge about their afflictions. He was rich in the Northern county currency of roguish eccentricity and independence. After the elopement, Dolly sought to mollify her furious parents for the lowly marriage by saying, 'His actions are so singular, and his spirits so manly and enterprising, that I could not help liking him.' The Metcalfs named their first son Christopher after Dolly's father, and were forgiven before too long.

Jack was the archetypal lovable rogue. He made friends easily, often out of those who tried to play on his blindness and bravado by drawing him into wagers. He'd bet on cards, bowls or any form of sport which offered itself provided there was some means of ensuring his chances, such as a trusted landlord to check the cards weren't marked. He wasn't above the odd sly tactic – engaging in bowls for which he scored three points for his opponent's one, he bribed observers to indicate the necessary alterations in aim through a code of raising or lowering their tones of voice. It was still a fair achievement when he won, though! He took part in a horse race where massive odds were laid against him (for fairly obvious reasons) on a mile-long course through woodland. Jack obtained four dinner bells and stationed friends at the course markers to prevent him losing his way. They were no doubt well rewarded when he won the race.

Jack sought out more lucrative lines of work to support his growing family. He bred horses, bought and sold them through his own 'braille-like' judgement and could spot weaknesses in them that the sighted could not always find. He taught his horses to neigh in response to their names, but he could still feel out his own in a herd of strangers. He bought and drove a successful stagecoach between York and Knaresborough until more moneyed locals stole the idea, and the trade. He went to sea, became a fish merchant and, as if that wasn't enough effort for one life, he became a soldier in 1745, marching North with 140 men he himself had recruited to join in squashing the Second Jacobite Rebellion. When his friend was captured, Jack infiltrated the enemy camp to find him.

It was another ten years before Jack embarked upon the civil engineering career that would give him a place in history as the first great road builder of the Industrial Revolution. He spotted an opportunity to apply his detailed knowledge of boggy moorland routes when the 1765 Turnpike Act authorised trusts to build toll roads in Yorkshire. Scarcely anyone had road building experience to match his understanding of the area and he won a contract to build three miles of road between Harrogate and Boroughbridge. The terrain was appalling and had defied all attempts at providing a civilised surface until then.

An earlier tale of classic Jackishness illustrates the dreadful road conditions in meeker landscapes than this one. His patron, a Colonel Liddell from his fiddle-playing days, once offered him a lift between London and Harrogate, which Jack declined, saying that with the state of the roads he could make the 190 miles faster on his own feet. Naturally, with his usual creative determination, he did. All his life he had been engaged in activities which involved travel and transport and he didn't need to see the roads to appreciate how deplorable they were.

Jack's 30-year career as a road builder of distinction came before Thomas Telford and John McAdam. He constructed over 180 miles of road, always on time (a skill which seems to have disappeared from modern road engineering) and within budget. He specialised in laying roads across bogs and marshland that traditional road makers had hitherto thought impossible. Self-taught upstarts often devise methods outside the box, and Jack fitted this mould. No stranger to rain, he knew that drainage was essential to a maintainable road and devised a technique for building smooth convex surfaces which swiftly drained into good ditches. These cambered surfaces were supported beneath on rafts made of tightly bound bundles of furze and ling. He earned a serious reputation and a formidable amount of money, £65,000 all told, completing his last road at the age of 75.

At 77 he walked to York to meet with a publisher and dictate an account of his life and then settled down in Spofforth with his daughter, where he superintended the farm until his death in 1810 at the age of 93. According to S. Baring-Gould's account, Jack Metcalf left four children, twenty grandchildren and over ninety great- and great-great-grandchildren. It seems to me he lived just about enough life himself for all of them put together. What a guy!

LAUNCELOT BLACKBURNE, THE SWASHBUCKLING ARCHBISHOP

1724

The Archbishop of York is second only to the Archbishop of Canterbury as the highest-ranking cleric in the Church of England. The Primate of England – strangely, his boss in Canterbury is the Primate of 'All England' – is enthroned in the ancient, noble York Minster and has his residence at Bishopthorpe Palace in the bonny village of Bishopthorpe. 'Thorpe' is a Middle English name for a hamlet, coming from the Old English/Norse word for village. Put another way, this lofty position has been around for a long time, and the reason for the Archbishop of York's importance in the church is tied historically to the days when York was the significant Roman capital of Britain. One way or another it is a long-standing, thoroughly respectable post.

There have been some unusual archbishops in spite of this. Cardinal Thomas Wolsey, in the early 1500s, held the post for 16 years without ever once entering the city of York. This was not altogether his fault: he was kept very busy for most of this time running Henry VIII's foreign policy, before being arrested for treason (for failing to secure the King's divorce) and dying on his way back to London to face the charges. One of his predecessors, Archbishop Richard le Scrope, didn't fare much better at the hands of the Henrys. He was beheaded for treason by Henry IV, although his devotion to the church held firm in his last request to be struck five times by the executioner's blade, once for each of the wounds of Christ. The current Archbishop, John Tucker Mugabi Sentamu, is also unusual. Born into Uganda's ancient Buffalo clan in 1949, he moved to Britain in the early 1970s and was priest in charge of

St Saviour, Brixton Hill, before becoming Bishop of Stepney in 1996. With a keen legal brain, he was adviser to the Stephen Lawrence Inquiry and the Damilola Taylor murder review, and has been a harsh critic of institutional racism in the police force. Sentamu had his own illustrative reasons for this stance, being the only bishop to have been stopped and searched by police, not once, but eight times! He caused controversy in 2012 by becoming a columnist in the new *Sun on Sunday*, a move which shocked many after the phone-hacking scandal and the fall of its predecessor, the *News of the World*.

So, Archbishops of York seem to have a tradition of making waves of one form or another, but Launcelot Blackburne was in a league of his own. He not only made waves, he sailed on them for part of his career – and not a very religious part at that! Launcelot Blackburne was a pirate of the Caribbean.

This colourful character was born in 1658 and graduated from Christchurch Oxford in 1680 and set off for the West Indies as soon as he was ordained. Once there, he spent four years on the high seas aboard a buccaneer ship, ostensibly as chaplain, although records of the time show that he made a fair sum of money, and not for swabbing the souls of his shipmates! Buccaneers had a confused status in terms of legal legitimacy, being quietly approved of in some ways by the English throne for their harrying of Spanish shipping. As pirates, they were too wild to be trusted, but were occasionally rewarded for services to the Crown. Launcelot Blackburne received the sum of £20 from Charles II in 1681, appearing in records as a payment for 'secret services'. What those secret services may have been is not elucidated, but twenty quid was a lot of money in those days and it is safe to assume these services were probably decidedly dodgy in 'man-of-the-cloth' terms.

Blackburne returned to England in 1684, when he made a very good match, marrying Catherine Talbot of Stourton Castle in Staffordshire. He became Archbishop of York in 1724, although he spent very little time in his diocese, preferring his London pad in Downing Street and the Royal Court for entertainment. He was keen on politics but ignored his more spiritual duties. He was said to have secretly married George I to his mistress and to have told

Queen Caroline she was a wise lass for not sulking over her husband's high-profile shenanigans.

As an archbishop who loved the ladies, this topic was obviously important to him: Blackburne had his own mistress, a Mrs Conwys, living with him and his wife, and was said to prefer at least a pair of young women on hand in his bedchamber. Once thrown out of church by the vicar of St Mary's in Nottingham, when he paused in the middle of a confirmation to call for ale and his pipe and tobacco, it is clear that his swashbuckling ways carried through into his new role. Blackburne was full to the gunwales with charm, a fine-looking man with barrels of wit and little or no moral fibre to speak of. He is described in Brewer's *Rogues, Villains and Eccentrics* as having 'behaviour ... seldom of a standard to be expected of an archbishop [and] in many respects his behaviour was seldom of a standard to be expected of a pirate'. He gave up ordaining priests not long after he was enthroned and could no longer be bothered with confirmations. It seems that he was generally more carnally occupied of a Sunday morning!

A HELL OF A LOT MORE
THAN FOUR-AND-TWENTY
BLACKBIRDS
1788

Pies, quite rightly, have a hallowed place on Yorkshire tables. Allowing for some variation of opinion as to crust, consistency, meat to potato ratio and so on, the difference between a good pie and a poor one can make or break a social occasion. It is an accepted currency for repaying favours, provided the maker is known to have a proven talent for pastry, and celebrations are lacking if no crust-crested monster is there, moored like a battleship amid the smaller sails of sandwiches.

The Yorkshire Christmas Pie was popular in Victorian times as a cut-and-come-again commodity to treat large numbers of poorer members of the parish, but is seldom attempted in modern Yorkshire kitchens. It is a mammoth undertaking, involving about three days of wrestling, de-boning and encapsulating a range of game and poultry, one inside the other: a partridge, a chicken, a duck, a goose and a turkey. Bolstered between layers with a forcemeat of hare, it comes out in compacted meaty stripes of light and dark, from its tanking of fat and flour. The ingredients list sounds a bit like the words to 'The Twelve Days of Christmas', although anyone attempting to reproduce this dish should be aware that it is not legal to put Lords-a-leaping in the oven and five gold rings could risk expensive dental bills among the guests.

When King George III recovered from mental illness in 1788 the Yorkshire village of Denby Dale decided to make a commemorative pie – a huge one! The success of the first Denby Dale Pie resulted in a tradition which has continued from generation to generation, with each subsequent pie bigger than the last. The second pie was made in 1815 to celebrate Napoleon's defeat at Waterloo. An army marches on its stomach, the short French general famously said, and this pie would have gone a long way towards feeding a battalion, at two feet deep and seven feet across. The 1846 pie, in honour of the Corn Law repeal, was such a brute that the platform that briefly supported it buckled under the strain, sending a meaty avalanche towards the waiting crowd, who rushed forward to meet it with knives and forks. This wasn't the worst disaster to befall a Denby Dale Pie, however; but the blame for the next one rests firmly out of county.

In 1887 came Queen Victoria's Golden Jubilee, as good a reason as any to improve on past efforts, so to ensure a solid base a local company fashioned a special dish from iron and steel for the princely sum of one hundred pounds. A fancy London chef was commissioned to oversee the bakers and ensure a particularly fine creation. After all, a ton and a half of meat and potatoes takes some cooking. Alas, he got it wrong, and when the pie was opened it was found to be rotten, causing the rather rowdy crowd that year to fall back, more effectively than if they had been peppered with rubber bullets. The pie festival turned into a funeral and the putrid remains were consigned to the earth, complete with dish, and covered with quicklime. The women saved the honour of the village by making a new pie themselves, three days later. It was named 'The Resurrection Pie', and was a lighter meal than the others, for only 2,000 people, containing merely a cow, two calves and a couple of sheep. It might have contained the fancy London chef if he hadn't fled on a train back to London the night before the great pie fiasco, probably aware that he had seriously messed up with his rotten southern creation!

There have so far been ten pies in Denby Dale, with occasional smaller setbacks, such as having to knock down the barn in which one 18-footer was made in order to get it out, and the tragic deaths of the four main organisers in 1964, who were killed in a car crash in the early hours of the morning on the way back from filming a programme about the pie for ITV. It was strange that the 1964 pie, which was to celebrate four royal births, took four lives as well. Some have suggested that the pie is inauspicious, citing the beginning of the tradition (in honour of the King recovering his mental health) as the cause of the bad luck, since the pie had barely been digested before he went mad again. Still, this is Yorkshire, and pie is pie, so on they go, the 1988 pie having made it into the *Guinness World Records*. This whale of a creation served a staggering 90,000 people over a period of two days. The most recent, made to celebrate the new millennium, weighed in at 12 tons, was 40 feet long and people from all over the world turned up to help eat it.

GENTLEMAN JACK –
AN EXCEPTIONAL FELLOW
1791

Anne Lister, born in 1791 and sometimes referred to as 'the first modern lesbian', would have disappeared into the mists of time if not for her spectacular diaries, all four million words of which lay concealed for more than a century behind panelling at her family seat of Shibden Hall, near Halifax. Anne wrote one sixth of her massive output (the saucy bits) in a code of her own devising, made up of algebraic symbols and Ancient Greek characters. Towards the end of the nineteenth century, the diaries were discovered and the code cracked by her successor John Lister (the last inhabitant of the hall) and his associate, Arthur Burrell. As the content of the secret passages unfurled into a tapestry of sapphic seductions and intimate self-reflection, Burrell advised his friend to burn the lot. Sensibly, and fortunately for posterity, John Lister ignored this advice and returned the 26 volumes to their hiding place, preserving a singular and detailed record of an extraordinary life for publication in a more accepting era. Extracts from the diaries were edited and published by Helena Whitbread in 1988.

Anne inherited Shibden Hall from her maiden aunt and uncle. They were well-respected local landowners, with 400 acres of estate dating back more than 300 years. Neither had married, but they raised Anne, and though at times shocked by her eccentric character, they loved her, finding much diversion in listening to her escapades. She had declared early on in their quest for suitors that she did not want a husband, that she intended to run the estate herself as well as any man, and she switched for a while from her lifelong study of the classics to books on engineering and farm management.

Anne's early relationship with Marianna Belcombe takes up a hefty number of diary pages. They were in love, but Marianna had other concerns – little or no personal fortune meant a lack of security that a good-looking gentlewoman could only resolve one way. Anne was horrified when, amid their repeated confessions of undying devotion, Marianna became engaged to a well-to-do older man, Charles Lawton. From the day of Marianna's marriage, Anne wore only black, an eccentric statement which gradually became more pronounced. Her predilection for masculine fitted jackets, high collars, stocks and hats, along with the rumours of her sex life that circulated freely around the alehouses of Shibden, earned her the nickname 'Gentleman Jack'.

Her relationship with Marianna continued for some years after the marriage – even, for a period, with the husband's tolerance. Marianna lacked Anne's independence of spirit, however, and found her friend's style of dress and public displays of attention embarrassing. There were rows. Still, she continued the affair with promises that her ageing husband would die presently and she would move to Shibden as soon as he did. When Anne realised her lover was seriously exaggerating Charles' state of decrepitude she finally broke off the relationship.

Though she had many flirtations and affairs in England and Paris, keeping a tally of the night's 'kisses' (orgasms) in her journals, what Anne really wanted was a wife. She knew her own self very well and was not merely exploring sex with other women in the absence of any other kind. She wrote, 'I love and only love the fairer sex and thus beloved by them in turn, my heart revolts from any love but theirs.'

Dalliances of a very discreet nature between women were not particularly disapproved of at that time and in some ways were seen as a positive means for maidens to gain some pre-marital experience and improve performance for their future husbands; but this was Regency England, a time when Jane Austen's virtuous beauties were setting their stalls out as domestic companions to respectable men of fortune. Dignity and decorum were of paramount importance and any whiff of unconventional behaviour could cause teacups to quiver in well-held saucers and lorgnettes to swoop up and settle beneath the raised eyebrows of dowagers in drawing rooms.

Anne cared little for this. As a gentleman, her life would have been thoroughly approved of – she was a good shot, she ran her estate, and in 1832 she made a good match with a wealthy heiress, Ann Walker, who moved in as her companion. Two years later, the ladies devised their own 'marriage' ceremony and exchanged rings to seal their union. Walker was reserved and shy, the feminine side of the duo whose dowry, as it were, contributed generously to the improvements Lister effected on her estate. They stayed together until Lister caught a serious fever while they were travelling in the foothills of the Caucasus and died in Koutaisi, Georgia. It took Walker seven months to have her lover's body embalmed and to bring her home to be buried in Yorkshire.

Since the discovery of Anne Lister's diaries, much attention has been given to her sexuality and her often very explicit descriptions of seductions. However, her other achievements, alongside these exploits, are unusual enough for the time: she remodelled and improved the Shibden estate; as a keen mountaineer, she became the first woman to climb several peaks in the Pyrenees; she opened and ran her own very successful colliery; she promoted education for girls in her region; and she travelled extensively.

Opinion is divided in summaries of her life. She is sometimes presented as a deceitful and predatory philanderer who seduces and drops one woman while taking up with the next. Others characterise her rather as so charming and gentle in her attentions as to have no need for roguish tactics. Anne was accepted and respected socially for much of her life, despite awareness of her sexual tastes, suggesting they were not regarded as particularly scandalous. Disapproval did not rest on this issue, rather it was used to fan the flames when neighbouring landowners found other aspects of her way of life a threat. The real reason for any unpopularity lies in the uncompromising challenge Anne presented to what was firmly regarded as male territory. She didn't curry favour, she didn't care whether she was liked as a woman, she flaunted her independence, and why the hell not? She was a landowner, she 'married' well, improved her property and took it forward into industrial profit. She was actually guilty of being a woman who behaved like a man, and excelling at it. Good on her!

THE WALLS OF YORK – SECURED SINCE AD 71, FINALLY DEFEATED BY A LITTLE GIRL

1797

The city of York has a history of being protected by perimeter walls dating back to the arrival of the Romans in AD 71. They built the original rectangular fortified camp covering 50 acres of ground on the banks of the River Ouse. The Danes took over in 867 and rebuilt the walls, retaining one tower of the somewhat dilapidated Roman fortifications. The Multangular Tower is still there to this day, although much of the remaining wall dates from the twelfth and fourteenth centuries. A huge part of the atmospheric charm of this once mighty city, the walls are now a scheduled monument and classified as a Grade I listed building. They have mutated along with the name of the city and have similarly retained features of their predecessors in a consistent traceable thread. In the time of the Roman occupation York retained its Celtic name Eboracum, which was subtly transformed for the Anglo-Saxon palate around AD 400 into Eoforwic or 'wild boar town'. When the Vikings came along the name morphed again into a Norse word which sounded appropriately similar: Jorvik, which means 'horse bay'. In its various incarnations the city walls, which took a serious beating in the Norman Conquest of 1066 and again in the Civil War when they were besieged by parliamentary forces in 1644, survived, rallying many times only to be finally opened for evermore when a strange occurrence broke their defences in 1797.

There are several gates in the walls of York, of which the Micklegate is the principal one, dating back to the 1570s. The gates, or 'bars' as they are known in reference to the simple but sturdy barriers used in quaint old times, were locked at night to prevent strangers entering the confines of the city. They were also manned when open and used for the collection of tolls from outsiders wishing to enter to sell in the city's markets. Yorkshire people have never been fond of 'comers-in' or 'off-comers', a tradition to which anyone moving to Yorkshire from another county can testify. It takes an average of about 30 years for one's outsider status to wear off and even then it's not guaranteed merely through the passing of time. Traders approaching the Micklegate Bar on market days would have their wares inspected and would be required to pay a tax per item before entering to sell. Over time, the bars became increasingly elaborate and the Micklegate was the scene of many ceremonial events. Traitors' heads adorned its top from time to time, traditionally skewered on pikestaffs. Among others, the head of Richard Plantagenet, father of Edward IV and Richard III, was put on display after the Battle of Wakefield in 1460. It was replaced in 1461 after the Battle of Towton with the heads of Lancastrian opposition leaders, illustrative of the notoriously messy Wars of the Roses that raged back and forth for 30 years in a bitter struggle for the throne of England. It is customary for kings and queens to knock at the Micklegate Bar and request permission to enter the inner sanctum of York. This has become something of a formality rather than a necessity since the gates are no longer locked.

The Micklegate Bar is a four-storey building with accommodation above the arch. Towards the end of the eighteenth century it was home to gatekeeper Thomas Brocklebank and his family. On her birthday, daughter Sarah had her little friends round to play and somehow, as birthdays often do, it all ended in tears. Sarah lost the gate key during the festivities and when her father came to lock the gate at dusk it was still missing. Thomas Brocklebank used a beam of wood to wedge the gate shut that night and charged Sarah with finding the key at all costs. When she failed, Thomas lost his job and the family were turned out of their home. Sarah's father was unforgiving and never spoke to her again, and such was the impact on her that she devoted her life to searching for the lost key.

Here the tale moves from simple fact into a more 'legend has it' kind of territory. Legend has it that Sarah was well known around the city, scouring rubbish heaps and wall chinks for any sign of the missing key. Forty years later she is said to have burst in on the Mayor of York as he was entertaining guests to declare that the key was found. Before divulging any useful information as to its whereabouts, however, Sarah had a heart attack and died on the spot. The Micklegate Bar remains unlocked and its upper floors now contain a museum, where even sensible-looking curators confirm that the building is haunted by little cold hands that unnerve visitors and, of course, by the triumphant jangling of found keys.

THE FIRST LADY JOCKEY BY 150 YEARS

1804

Riding side-saddle is one of the many historical handicaps women have had to put up with in the race with men. For hundreds of years it was seen as thoroughly indecorous for a lady to straddle a horse, although there were some exceptions: Marie Antoinette was known to ride astride, as was Catherine the Great of Russia, who wore a man's military tunic to complete the look. Still, if you were Empress of all Russia, you could pretty much do as you liked, and given her sexual appetite there probably weren't that many subjects around at court who had difficulty picturing her straddling anything!

It was not until the 1830s that Jules Pellier designed a side-saddle with two pommels, finally giving women a decent chance at control and movement, despite the ongoing encumbrance of voluminous, buffeting skirts … but that was after Alicia Meynell's time. She became the first ever female English jockey in 1804, nearly 150 years before the next would come along. Until the 1940s, she was the only woman in the history of the Jockey Club to have raced against a man and won.

Alicia Meynell was a beautiful and charming woman with blonde tresses, bright blue eyes and that all-important feature of female loveliness, a cheek with a roseate hue. She was not born in Yorkshire, but followed her sister's example and married into the county. Her husband, the rather dashing Lieutenant-Colonel Thomas Thornton of the York Militia, was a neighbour of her sister's husband, William Flint. They were all horse mad. Alicia was an unusually talented rider with a bold spirit and a good 'seat', and she kept three hunters, riding to hounds in a time when this was still a rare pursuit for women. Much as modern-day petrol-heads vie for supremacy in cars, Alicia got into an argument while out riding with her brother-in-law over who was riding the best steed. She was mounted on her husband's horse, a great fiery beast by the name of Vingarillo, while Flint was riding his own spectacular hunter, Thornville. Much snorting and prancing ensued and they decided to settle it with a race. Alicia beat Flint, not once, but twice. This didn't sit well with the vanquished relative, who challenged her to a proper race, on a proper track, for proper prize money. Carrying an unusual amount of concealed testosterone for such a comely young lady, Alicia accepted and the challenge was set for the last day of the York races in August of that year, with a whopping prize of 1,000 guineas, payable by the loser.

The challenge generated enormous interest in the racing community, and a crowd of 100,000 people is said to have turned out to see this novelty. The 6th Light Dragoons had to be brought in to hold the throng of spectators in check, but nothing was in place to hold back the gambling, and bets were flying round to the tune of £200,000, a vast sum for the time. Mrs Thornton appeared on the track in a fabulous, leopardy get-up of buff-coloured spotted skirts, with cute blue sleeves and matching cap. Her beauty, her style and her horsemanship immediately secured the affection of the audience, but Flint was not impressed, and made sure she was on the side of the track that would incommode her whip hand and give him the advantage, as if riding astride wasn't advantage enough. All the same, Alicia was ahead for three-quarters of the race, until Vingarillo faltered in the last mile of the four-mile circuit and Flint overtook and won. The social victory was hers, however, and she went on to win two other races that season, although the local papers seemed unsure which to most admire her for: her spectacular side-saddle style, or her beautifully embroidered purple stockings.

The stockings may have been fabulous, the horsemanship certainly was, but the husband, Colonel Thornton, was a major disappointment. He refused to honour the wager after the race with Flint, claiming it had just been a bit of fun. This so angered his brother-in-law that on the day of Alicia's next race, Flint turned up with a horse whip and flayed Thornton beside the track, ending up in gaol for assault. This was nothing, however, compared to Thornton's later conduct towards his wife. He travelled to France in

1814 and never returned, and on his death, ten years later, it was found he had left most of his estate to a Priscilla Duins, with whom he had been living the while. He left Alicia nothing and gave their son a measly token gesture of £100. In his time with Priscilla, Thornton had had a daughter, who was well provided for in his will and who, in a curious twist of historical detail, was named Thornvillia, after the horse his rejected wife had raced against and which belonged to the friend he had slighted. Strange man!

THE YORKSHIRE WITCH – EXECUTED
1809

Mary Bateman was a serial confidence trickster. She just couldn't stop herself. Even while locked in York Castle, about to meet her end, she managed to diddle her cellmate out of the last of her cash. Her nefarious methods of 'healing' her victims often resulted in their deaths. She earned the title 'The Yorkshire Witch', purporting to be familiar with the arts of charms, spells and fortune-telling, and this in return earned her a gruesome end. Her skeleton (what's left of it) is in the Thackray Medical Museum in Leeds.

She was born Mary Harker, the daughter of a North Yorkshire farmer, and went into service in Thirsk at the age of 13. Her pilfering ways went undiscovered until she moved to York, a city she had to flee when she was connected to a robbery. She moved to Leeds, where she married an uninspired, hard-working man, John Bateman, in 1792. Bateman then worked for a while as a dressmaker, earning far more from susceptible clients than she could have done merely for the dresses she made, helping to lighten their purses by playing on their superstitions. Devoid of moral boundaries of any kind, she falsified a letter around this time, telling her husband that his father was dying. He hastened away to the bedside of a perfectly healthy parent, only to return to Leeds to find his workshop had been mysteriously emptied of tools. His charming wife had pawned the lot. This experiment led to several similar shaftings in the same mould.

Over the years, she fine-tuned her skills to include fortune-telling and the concocting of potions to ward off evil spirits or retrieve lost loved ones. She often created her own market in this respect, preying on people's insecurities; inventing extramarital affairs with nonexistent women, for instance, to give a cause for her services.

In one case, when a neighbour died, leaving his children with their stepmother, Bateman convinced her that the oldest son had plans to deprive her of his father's money. She suggested the widow should sell up everything, leave the children, and move away. This she did, entrusting our Mary with a sum of money for the children's care; Mary kept the cash and sent the children to the workhouse.

Another tactic was to encourage the use of charms, which involved sewing valuables into bags inside mattresses to ward off evils. The victims felt secure in the knowledge that their possessions were safe beneath them as they slept, doing good work against the dark forces, until they had doubts and sneaked a look, finding scrap paper instead of pound notes and pennies instead of sovereigns. When challenged about this Bateman was quite unruffled, pointing out that they had broken the spell by looking and had turned all to dust with their doubts. It is incredible how long she got away with these antics, although she moved house often and lived in superstitious times. Her reputation grew as a spiritual aid to those in need, even though she was already killing people with her increasing collection of poisons, working her way so far into their confidence that by the time they died from her 'assistance', she was left with the keys to their house and had time to fence everything before relatives or creditors arrived. Scams came readily to Mary's mind. A huge fire in a factory, which caused many injuries, was a fine opportunity to pose as a nurse and go from door to door collecting for the unfortunates. More than one lonely woman ended up in the poorhouse after giving Bateman all they had to alleviate their suffering.

Her final undoing was occasioned by her dealings with a couple called Perigo. She played husband and wife off against each other mercilessly, convincing them that an evil lay over their union, which (after she'd had £70 and half their furniture off them) was only curable by a six-day course of puddings, into which they were to bake a series of palliative powders. Bafflingly, they went from excellent health to death's door under Bateman's supervision, without suspecting her at all. It was only when the wife died in agony that the husband began to smell a rat. With what was left of his strength, Perigo called in the authorities, and in October 1808 Bateman was arrested on suspicion of fraud and later charged with Rebecca Perigo's murder.

Horrified crowds attended the trial, and after Bateman had stepped into oblivion, unrepentant, she was cut down and taken to Leeds Infirmary, where an even larger crowd was assembled to see the 'Yorkshire Witch'. The hospital earned some useful funds, charging thruppence a head to view the hated corpse, and around 2,500 people paid to see it. Mary Bateman's skin was flayed and tanned and sold off in strips, to ward off evil spirits!

MOONRAKERS AND CUCKOOS
1810

I went to school in the Colne Valley where the local accent, opaque as it is to outsiders, was distinct from one village to another. You didn't need a postcode to tell a Marsden child from a Slaithwaite child even though these two rural villages are a hop, skip and a jump from one another along the canal towpath. Proximity and similarity were all that was needed to keep the two discrete. In true Yorkshire tradition, each village regards the next as daft for very similar reasons, which these two strange tales illustrate: the Slaithwaite Moonrakers and the Marsden Cuckoos.

In the early nineteenth century, as the need for industrial transportation grew, the Huddersfield Narrow Canal was built along the Colne Valley. Trade flourished and for some time laden narrow boats passed through Slaithwaite in a continuous stream. Less official water trafficking flourished too, with smugglers paddling quiet-oared under the shadowy banks at night. On one occasion, customs men from neighbouring Marsden were spotted approaching from the lock as a local gang were offloading a cargo of liquor. The gang stowed their barrels amid the reeds and made off to wait until the coast was clear. Much later in the night they returned with rakes to raise the barrels under a moonless stormy sky of clouds. The customs officials were waiting and surprised the gang, demanding an account of what they were up to. Some impressive quick-thinking on the part of one of the smugglers explained that they were worried the moon had fallen into the canal and were raking it out to return it to the heavens. The officials are said to have been so taken with this proof of the rival village's stupidity that they returned to Marsden, howling with laughter. The barrels were retrieved and there was quite a party in Slaithwaite, no doubt laced with similar mirth as much as with pots of moonshine.

To emphasise the looking-glass nature of these two villages, Marsden is known for the cuckoo legend. The village is higher up the Colne Valley than Slaithwaite and is only accessible from the lower end, being surrounded on three sides by the high hills of Marsden Moor, Meltham Moor and Saddleworth Moor. The wildly beautiful barren moorland is nowadays mostly in the care of the National Trust and is a wonderful place for walking, cycling and contemplation. However, in times gone by this was a cruel place to live out harsh winters and the arrival of spring was quite literally a life-saver. Even now, in the days of Gore-Tex and self-defrosting windscreens, the signs of spring, snowdrops and crocuses are a great lift to the spirits around these hills. As swallows are said to herald the arrival of summer, the cuckoo traditionally aired its first distinctive mating call of the year on 24 April, marking Marsden's spring cattle fair. Of course, the cuckoo doesn't set its calendar quite so precisely but it is still heard in the area at this time of year.

The story of the Marsden cuckoo has several variations on the same theme, mainly that the local people were so desperate to keep winter away, they devised a Baldrick-style cunning plan to keep the cuckoo in situ. As it sang in the field, they worked to raise the height of the wall around it, but the noise scared the cuckoo into flight. Some bright spark is said to have noticed that the cuckoo brushed the top of the wall as it flew away, causing this comment on the construction – 'It were nobbut just one course too low'.

The canal connecting these two villages, which had operated for 140 years, was abandoned in 1944 when a rail link destroyed its commercial value. After much controversy and 27 years of campaigning it was re-opened to the sole use of leisure craft, helping to recreate these now mill-less communities as fashionable and picturesque locales for affluent commuters to enjoy village life. The traditions have similarly been re-vitalised. Both villages have thriving festivals attended by thousands of people to celebrate their respective tales. And both continue to affectionately mock each other for their respective legendary stupidity.

MODERN CIVILISATION –
IT ALL BEGAN IN LEEDS
1811

Where else? The idea that everything of value to the modern world comes from God's Own County is a favourite among staunch Yorkshire types, an argument often based on the invention of three things in Leeds: rail transport, Portland cement and motion pictures. These three innovations – ease of transportation, mass-construction capabilities and film – have been hugely influential in the creation of our society today.

Nineteenth-century England was a golden era for discovery and innovation, when the seeds that revolutionised industry, leisure, health and mobility began to grow in earnest. In 1812 John Blenkinsop designed the first successful steam railway locomotive to run between Middleton Colliery and Leeds. The major shortage of horses and feeds occasioned by the drain of the Napoleonic War made alternative power increasingly important. Blenkinsop gained the edge over competitors with his use of edge rails, which were made of iron, rather than the customary plated wooden ones. Richard Trevithick, in Cornwall, had had to abandon his valuable work on an effective colliery locomotive for lack of rails strong enough to support his weighty creations, and Blenkinsop forged ahead. He defied the commonly held belief that a locomotive could only be expected to pull four times its own weight, and that only in ideal weather conditions. He devised a rack and pinion system, using a geared wheel that locked into a toothed rack beside the rail, and his engine routinely pulled a payload of 90 tons, around 18 times its own weight. The Middleton Railway was a great success, and is now the oldest continually running railway in the world.

Ordinary Portland Cement (OPC) is the most common cement used in modern construction and is regarded as originating from Leeds bricklayer Joseph Aspdin in the 1820s, although it was actually one of his employees who got the recipe right. OPC gets its name from Portland stone because of the similarity in appearance between the two. It is the fundamental ingredient for mortar and concrete worldwide, allowing buildings to rise far more rapidly than with traditional mortars.

Louis Le Prince, regarded by many film historians as the true founder of motion pictures, conducted his ground-breaking work in Leeds in 1888, using a single-lens camera of his own ingenious design. His two films, *Leeds Bridge* and *Roundhay Garden Scene*, were made several years before the work of his more famous competitors, the Lumiére brothers and Thomas Edison, produced anything that actually resembled a film. Sadly Le Prince never got to make his major public demonstration due to his mysterious disappearance from a train in France in 1890. He said goodbye to his brother on a platform in Dijon, boarded the Paris express and completely vanished. Neither his body nor his luggage were ever found. His widow and son were convinced that some foul play was involved, given the competitive nature of Le Prince's research, and his intention to patent the camera when he reached his journey's end. However, despite the best efforts of police in France and Britain, no clue was found and the case was never cleared up. More than a hundred years later, a picture of a drowned man, who bore some resemblance to Le Prince, was discovered in a French police archive, but it was far from conclusive. Theories abound, ranging from suicide, fratricide or a cunning plan to avoid debts, to a patent war turned seriously nasty. Nobody knows what happened, but it is curious that his son, who worked closely with him and went to America to try and push for his father to be properly acknowledged for his achievement, was reported as having tragically managed to blow his own head off while duck hunting near New York city.

I have enjoyed many discussions that have upheld Yorkshire as being significant in the development of just about everything the modern world has to offer, although the occasional suggestion that the development of New Orleans jazz has nothing to do with African rhythm, but is a product of clog dancing, is going a bit too far. I have seen clog dancing performances and, trust me, the debate stops right there.

THE LUDDITES, WHAT THEY STOOD FOR, AND THE BRONTË CONNECTION
1812

The term 'Luddite' is a well-known one and yet it is often misappropriated. In the modern world people declare themselves to be Luddites if they can't upload a file or type a text message in less than 30 minutes, believing the followers of the mythical General Ludd to have been technophobic dolts who wished to deny progress. In reality, the Luddites were a non-political movement of highly skilled textile workers, well above average in terms of machine-operating technical savvy. What they objected to was not technology itself, but the way in which it was being used corrosively by some manufacturers, bent on dismantling the right of workers to an honest day's pay for an honest day's work.

The movement began in Nottingham in 1811 and had spread to the industrial towns of Lancashire, and more particularly Yorkshire, by the beginning of 1812. The Luddites specifically targeted mills they saw as being run aggressively with no regard whatsoever for the workers the new machines displaced. The members of this secret society sent out a warning first, demanding removal of the machines, and when the warning was not complied with, they instigated night-time raids with a kind of sledgehammer called an 'Old Enoch' to smash the frames that had replaced their artisan skills.

Not unlike the Yorkshire mining communities of the 1980s, they had strong local sympathy, but they were up against the impossible odds of powerful political agendas. The government had their reasons for the brutal quashing of the Luddite protests, which brought Britain dangerously close to revolution. The majority of the army were abroad for the Napoleonic Wars and the slump in trade occasioned by this and the War of 1812 with the United States meant that people up and down the country were experiencing privation. No food and no jobs produced a powder keg waiting for a spark, so an example had to be made of the Luddites. The Frame-Breaking Act of February 1812 hastily introduced the death penalty, specifically for these protesters, and militia were called in to further protect factory assets. However, the unemployed were desperate enough to risk the severe penalties. The famous attack on William Cartwright's mill, Rawfolds in Huddersfield, resulted in carnage, as Cartwright had arranged an ambush by armed troops. This stung the Luddites into retaliation and they upped their game accordingly, to include assassination, murdering William Horsfall, an outspoken anti-Luddite mill owner. Things began to subside in 1813, after 17 men were rounded up for their part in these events and hanged in York.

Charlotte Brontë described the attack on Rawfolds Mill in her novel *Shirley*. She changed the names but retained the details, having heard the story from her father, whose life was singularly affected by the incident. Before his children were born, he was vicar at Hartshead Moor, a quiet hamlet community on the hill above the more densely populated valley, where the Huddersfield authorities, fearful of Luddite activity, had stationed a garrison of 1,000 troops to counter any trouble. On the night of the Rawfolds attack, several hundred Luddites assembled in Cooper Bridge and took the lonely route across the moor to avoid early detection. Patrick Brontë heard the hundreds of feet pass his gate in the middle of the night and was so terrified by the experience that he bought himself a gun for protection. By the time Charlotte and her equally literary sisters came into the world, he still continued the custom of discharging it at dusk from the parsonage door, to keep it in working order. To emphasise confused attitudes towards the Luddites, it is said that when some of the injured men who fled from the disastrous attack on Rawfolds later died of their wounds, they were buried in unmarked graves at Hartshead Church, where Patrick Brontë turned a blind eye, making no objection, despite his fears of these same troubled men who had caused him to arm himself.

THE HAND OF GLORY
1824

Sitting in a museum, atop a salt-blown hill in Whitby, North Yorkshire, is the only known 'Hand of Glory' remaining in Britain. An essential part of a superstitious burglar's kit until the early nineteenth century, a Hand of Glory is a mummified human hand, severed at the wrist, and said to have magical powers.

Folklore tales and legends, as usual, give differing accounts of the power of these 'hands'. Common conceptions are that the hand could open locked doors and that if the bearer ignited it while reciting an enchantment, the hand could send all inhabitants of a dwelling into a deep unwakable sleep (useful for underhand deeds such as plundering and looting). Opinions on how to ignite a Hand of Glory vary. Some tales report that a candle made from the flesh of the original owner, wax and sesame should be placed in the clenched hand and lit, while others suggest that the actual fingers themselves are lit, but burglars beware: if one of the fingers refuses to light, or goes out, one of the inhabitants is not asleep! Another common belief was that a lit candle in the hand would shine only for the holder, allowing them to see in pitch-darkness while others could not even see the candle. This gave rise to claims that invisibility was one of its powers. It was also thought that you could only put out the flames on the hand with blood, or blue (skimmed) milk.

Descriptions can be found of how a Hand of Glory is made. Firstly, it must be severed at the wrist (purportedly from a felon, fresh from the gallows); it must then be wrapped and squeezed dry of all blood and fluids, before being placed in a jar of salt. After two weeks, it must be taken out, dusted off, and cooked until completely dried. Please don't try this at home!

The most common Hand of Glory tale is set on a barren moor in North Yorkshire. Accounts vary, and are often vague, with no particular locale, but two specific and quite detailed versions have survived. One, from 1797, relates to 'The Spital Inn' on Stainmore, and the other, from 1824, to 'The Oak Tree Inn' in Leeming, though they follow the same basic plot.

On a dark and stormy night (it is always a dark and stormy night, isn't it?) on a desolate Yorkshire moor, there is a knock on the door of an inn. Freezing and wet, a beggar enters, and pleads to be allowed to stay the night. The innkeeper has no spare beds but allows the beggar to sleep in front of the fire in the bar. The owner, staff and guests shortly retire to their beds, all but the cook, a young lass, who is awake in the back room. Able to view the beggar through a small pane of glass between the rooms, the cook witnesses the beggar pull a brown, withered, human hand from his pocket. He takes a match and, while incanting, lights the fingers of the hand one by one; each flames as if it were a candle. Filled with horror, the girl rushes up the back steps and tries to awaken her master and the other men of the house, but to no avail – they sleep a charmed sleep. Finding her efforts in vain, she goes back downstairs and watches through the window. All the fingers of the severed hand are lit, but not the thumb. The beggar moves around the property through locked and unlocked doors alike, putting things to his fancy into a sack. When he moves into yet another room the girl dashes to the hand and attempts to put out the flaming fingers. She throws a jug of beer over them, only for the flames to burn brighter; she tries water, but with no luck. In desperation she throws some milk and the flames are extinguished. The spell is broken! The innkeeper hears the girl's screeching and descends in time to detain the thief, who is later tried and hanged for his crimes.

Legends of 'Hands of Glory' have existed all across Europe for a span of over 400 years. Some believe its name actually derives from mandrake, a plant of the genus *Mandragora*, which is very similar to the French *main de gloire* – Hand of Glory. The root of the plant causes delirium and hallucinations, and in high doses it can even send the user into a coma. In moderation the chemicals present in the mandrake root produce brainwave activity similar to that found in REM sleep, and have for a long time been used as an anaesthetic. The mandrake plant is also said to be luminescent. Both properties lend themselves to the alleged capabilities of a Hand of Glory, as does the appearance of the roots, which sometimes resemble shrivelled human figures. Some legends state that when a mandrake is pulled from the earth, it lets out a scream deadly to all who hear it.

References to Hands of Glory have appeared in popular literature and modern big-screen films. Arguably the most famous of such appearances is in the magical adventures of Harry Potter. In J.K. Rowling's second book, *Harry Potter and the Chamber of Secrets*, the hand is on display in Borgin & Burkes – a shop of dark-natured magical curiosities. Borgin tells customers, 'Insert a candle and it gives light only to the holder. Best friend to thieves and plunderers.' The hand makes a second appearance in Rowling's sixth book of the series, *Harry Potter and the Half-Blood Prince*, where Draco Malfoy uses it to escape from the Room of Requirement, after application of 'Peruvian Instant Darkness Powder'. He then slips away using the light only he can see, while the others are in complete darkness. Coincidentally, mandrake roots and their properties also feature in the Harry Potter tales.

To this day, visitors to Whitby ponder the true capabilities (if any!) of the hand, with its ill-boding history and gaunt appearance. Did it bestow magical powers on its user, or was this belief in mystical superiority the reason why so many foolish hopefuls seem to have been caught while relying on these pickled mitts. What is it that draws our interest to the unexplained and supernatural? Fear and awe are closely linked. The Germans have a word for it, *ehrfurcht*, meaning 'reverence for that which we cannot understand'. The Hand of Glory is a bizarre relic worth a visit; you don't have to be a burglar to gaze at it and wonder.

AN ARSON ATTACK THAT RESULTED IN BEDLAM
1829

At 6 a.m. on 2 February 1829, choristers on their approach to York Minster noticed that the ground frost had suddenly disappeared, leaving warm stones beneath their feet. On looking up at the lofty vastness of their glorious Gothic cathedral, they saw sparks rising from the wooden roof, one of the largest in Europe and a monument to medieval engineering. A couple of steps further and heat radiating from the 71m high walls caused them to raise the alarm. Despite the furious efforts of fire-fighters and the people of York, the blaze was not extinguished until the middle of the following night; the roof was destroyed along with part of the interior beneath.

This was far and away the most spectacular case of arson in the history of Britain, real fire and brimstone stuff, as reports from the time tell of debris raining from the sky, blazing crossbeams crashing down into the choir and molten lead pouring from the spouting. The heart of this awe-inspiring cathedral was bared to the heavens and an investigation was already under way before the flames were beaten.

It didn't take long. Four letters in the same hand, all threatening divine retribution on men of the church, had been sent that winter. The letters, long, rambling and rather irritating in style of address, had not been taken seriously. This is hardly surprising given that on closer inspection it was revealed that, although purporting to be anonymous, the sender had included his initials and a return address. Jonathan Martin, a former Wesleyan preacher, was not at home when the authorities called. However, the investigation uncovered some interesting corroborative details on Mr Martin from neighbours, such as his threatening to shoot Edward Legge, the Bishop of Oxford, as a consequence of which he had been incarcerated in a lunatic asylum and had subsequently escaped twice – unfortunately he had only been re-apprehended once.

Prior to this incident Martin as a preacher had been known for his vehement denunciations of the Church of England. Following his designs on the life of the bishop and his committal to Gateshead Asylum, the Wesleyan Church expelled him from their order.

Jonathan Martin was born in 1782, one of 12 varyingly precocious children. His younger brother John Martin was the celebrated English Romantic painter, who, although very successful in his field, always preferred engineering – he drew up many innovative plans for London transport and sanitation that posthumously proved visionary as they came to fruition. Another brother, Richard, served in the Peninsular War and was present at the Battle of Waterloo. Yet another became the inventor William Martin, whose few excellent inventions were somewhat overshadowed by his quack creations and speeches against contemporary scientists and engineers he accused of stealing his ideas. Isaac Newton, Michael Faraday and George Stephenson were just some of the great innovators who got the same treatment from William as the church got from Jonathan.

One can't help wondering what went down at the Martin family dinner table when these boys were growing up. William Martin was known in adult life for declaiming while wearing a helmet he'd made from a tortoise's shell and Jonathan's childhood was certainly disturbed. He was raised amid regular old-school threats of hell and damnation; he witnessed his sister's murder at the hands of their neighbour when he was just a boy; and he was press-ganged into six years in the Royal Navy, where he sustained a blow to the head which reportedly augmented his mental instability. In 1828, the year before he ignited the Minster, he suffered a major breakdown.

At his trial for arson on 31 March 1829, Jonathan was obligingly forthcoming with the details of his crime, providing a full account of how he had concealed himself in shadows as the Minster emptied after evensong, then divided his time between praying and cutting strips of velvet and fringing from the bishop's pew with a razor before sparking his flint and feeding the flames with prayer books and cushions. He had then made his escape by breaking a window and letting himself down the outside of the Minster with a bell rope.

He gave this account with laughing good humour in spite of the courtroom being so mobbed with people of York intent on lynching him that the proceedings had to be delayed to make room for the lawyers and a detachment of yeomanry, present throughout to keep the peace.

Martin's successful brother, John, did not attend the embarrassing hearing, but provided him with excellent representation in the form of Henry Brougham, 1st Baron of Brougham and Vaux, who had eloquently represented Queen Caroline some years earlier. In spite of the wishes of the people of York that Martin should be hanged, the judge directed the jury to deliberate only on his mental state. It took them seven minutes to pronounce Martin insane and he was committed to the infamous Bethlam Lunatic Asylum – Bedlam, as it was 'affectionately' known – where he lived out his days with a cheerful smile and was well behaved until his death on 26 May 1838 at the age of 56.

After this devastating attack, York Minster established its own constabulary to patrol the building and keep constant watch over its safety, later given the title of Minster Police in 1855.

To this day, the Minster remains one of just seven cathedrals worldwide to have its own privately regulated police force. This did not protect it from one more curious incendiary incident that took place on 9 July 1984. The roof of the South Transept caught fire when it was struck by lightning, causing £2.5m-worth of damage. Strangely, many interpreted this as a comment from the Almighty on the ordaining there of the Bishop of Durham, David Jenkins, three days before. Jenkins' ordination had caused controversy due to allegations that he held heterodox beliefs. He was hounded for saying that the Resurrection was a 'conjuring trick with bones' although it seems, as is often the way with press fame, he was misquoted. Jenkins remained in office as bishop until 1994, and no further signs of divine wrath were visited on York Minster.

FOUR EXCEPTIONALLY WELL-MARRIED DAUGHTERS

1833

'It is a truth universally acknowledged, that a single man in possession of a good fortune must be in want of a wife.' This very famous opening sentence to Jane Austen's *Pride and Prejudice* introduces the theme prevalent in so many of her novels: that of marrying off intelligent, accomplished daughters, with little or no dowry to offer, as an inducement to suitors of social standing. But it was not just in Austen's time that this was of all-consuming importance to parents; it has run through hundreds of years of history. Even in modern, more equal society, this theme has proved a popular one and led recently in 2004 to the very successful transfer of the novel to Gurinder Chadha's Bollywood movie *Bride and Prejudice*, which reflects cultural similarities in a present-day Punjabi family.

This particular tale comes from the Victorian era, when the MacDonalds, a Yorkshire family with eleven children, seven of whom were daughters, faced the age-old problem. They moved around a lot in their early lives, as preachers' families did, mainly between Huddersfield and Sheffield. The MacDonalds were certainly middle class, but only just, commanding no social prestige and with very little money, and yet four of their daughters were spectacularly well married to influential men of their time. They ended up presiding at the tables of country houses and smart London establishments beyond their wildest dreams. Their respective husbands and sons collected knighthoods, baronetcies, awards and leadership of the arts; and, for one of them, leadership of the country itself.

Alice MacDonald married John Lockwood Kipling and moved to Bombay in what was then British India, where her son Rudyard was born. He was to become the first English-writing recipient of the Nobel Prize for literature and was also its youngest ever winner. He turned down a knighthood and the poet laureateship and was an influential, avant-garde and much-loved writer, best remembered for such works as his children's novel *The Jungle Book* and the poem 'If'.

Alice was known socially as a vivacious wit and she published her own poetry. The Viceroy of India at the time said of her, 'Dullness and Mrs Kipling cannot exist in the same room.' There is a similarity between the Kiplings and the modern-day Beckhams (although the latter couple are not known for their conversational brilliance): the Kiplings also named their first-born after the place where they courted; not Brooklyn in their case, but Rudyard Lake in Staffordshire.

Georgiana MacDonald married the leading pre-Raphaelite painter Edward Burne-Jones. She was a spirited, creative force involved in her own art work and she contested local elections the first time that women were permitted to stand. Her very successful husband became a baronet and the couple stayed together despite his destructive and passionate affair with his Greek model, Maria Zambaco. He was a close friend of William Morris from their Oxford days and it has been suggested that Morris and Georgiana had an affair as well.

These arty types had all sorts of complex emotional dealings that are hard to unravel. It is known that at the time of Burne-Jones' Greek affair, not only did Morris and Mrs Burne-Jones grow close, Morris' own wife Jane was in love with Rosetti! There was some sort of crisis point when Burne-Jones' model Maria tried to commit suicide by jumping in the Regent's Canal and this seems to have marked the end of the affair, which Burne-Jones described as 'the emotional climax of his life' and both marriages remained intact. Georgiana and William Morris stayed close friends until the end of their lives.

Agnes MacDonald was a beauty and became the wife of painter and Royal Academy president Edward Poynter. He was made the first Slade professor at University College London and received a knighthood. He was also appointed as director of the National Gallery in 1894, where he oversaw the opening of the Tate Gallery, and was made a baronet in 1902.

Louisa MacDonald wrote novels, poetry and short stories, and she married Alfred Baldwin, the industrialist and politician who was director of the Great Western Railway. Her only child was three-times prime minister Stanley Baldwin, first Earl Baldwin of Bewdley. Stanley Baldwin dominated the British government between the First and Second World Wars and was a Conservative like his father. He is the only prime minister to have served under three different monarchs – George V, Edward VIII and George VI. He was the first to explore the potential of new media such as film and radio for political campaigning, and a mover and a shaker of the early twentieth century.

The social success brought about through the MacDonald girls' marriages is perhaps best accounted for by the times they lived in. Their parents, George and Hannah, were married in 1833. George was a Methodist preacher with an income of no more than £150 per annum and although the job traditionally came with a house, he and his wife were blessed with such a steady flow of hale and hearty children, they more than filled their official residences. Still, they were flourishing years for Methodists in the North, where industrialisation had caused a massive migration from the countryside to the job-rich towns. Agricultural workers moving into industry were feeling the loss of a sense of community and, as a consequence, were drawn to the evangelical church. The religion thrived among the middle classes too as they in turn expanded to manage these hordes of post-bumpkin factory workers. These were exciting times in the North as this phenomenal influx of huge numbers of people opened up all sorts of social developments.

The MacDonald daughters were raised by a mother whose family had made their fortune in the wholesale business in Manchester. She didn't inherit any wealth, but had been unusually well educated and had learned music, Italian and an appreciation of the arts. Their father was a keen reader who filled the house with books, apart from Shakespeare, who the evangelicals of the time deemed as offering nothing more than an obscene catalogue of vice and vulgarity. Nevertheless, the MacDonald children were rambunctious and gregarious and liked to engage one another in witty repartee. The daughters were challenging and creative, as the family's surviving correspondence shows. A friend of their brother Harry, who called regularly at the house, entered a light-hearted bet with the sisters over whether he would dare to eat a mouse pie. Rash fool! The next time he called, he was presented with this appetising dish, the contents of which the sisters had gone to much personal trouble to catch and surround with pastry. According to the letters, the visitor balked at the challenge of tasting it, but the girls did not. It seems they won their bet!

Through careful economy the family saved enough to send their eldest son to university. He brought home a stream of friends, intellectual and talented young men from what was known as 'The Birmingham Set', who could not help taking to the refreshing archness of his sisters. It is remarkable that so many daughters in one modest family married so well; the MacDonald sisters were there for the last gasp of the Victorian era alongside men who were influential in shaping the cultural and political birth of the twentieth century.

WHIT WALKS, WAKES AND THE ONWARDNESS OF THE CHRISTIAN SOLDIERS

1865

The Christian festival of Pentecost is the seventh Sunday after Easter, known as Whitsuntide. Before the Industrial Revolution took our sheep-processing communities from rustic hovels to terraced slums, Whitsuntide was a farming holiday, a natural break in the agricultural calendar when farm workers could kick up their heels in the meadows. Although scholars have never quite settled on a satisfactory explanation for the origins of Whitsun, it is thought to be a contraction of 'White Sunday', a time when the maids of villages wore white dresses. It is mentioned as far back as the early thirteenth century and was a time for festivities such as fairs and pageants, for feats of strength and competitive events. One poster from 1778 advertises events to be held at Whitsun as follows:

> *In the afternoon a gold-laced hat worth 30s to be cudgell'd for; On Whit Tuesday, a fine Holland smock and ribbons to be run for by girls and young women. And in the afternoon six pairs of buckskin gloves to be wrestled for.*

This account sounds to me like a fair description of the January sales in the twenty-first century, but when the countrysiders became the inner-city dwellers, the lords of industry decided that the rowdiness and wassailing of their workers at Whitsuntide was inappropriate. They sought ways to encourage more dignified leisure pursuits, retaining the idea of smart new clothes, but removed from the fun aspect of cudgelling anyone for them.

Whit Monday became a formal bank holiday in 1871, and continued to be celebrated in Yorkshire by the church and chapel processions called Whit Walks. As industries grew, many of the walks became associated with a particular mill or colliery community. Given the necessity for a yearly overhaul of increasingly complex mill machinery, the factories closed at this time for their 'wakes', taking over the cycle of the agricultural break after planting for a round-the-clock spit and polish. The tradition held for everyone to get their annual set of new clothes in readiness for the processions, and families, however poor, would make sure their children looked smart, sometimes with the aid of wealthier members of the parish, who took great pride in their workers' or congregation's turnout at this event. Children would call at the houses of their neighbours and relatives to be congratulated on their fine appearance and, more importantly, to receive a penny, a custom which helped guarantee the involvement of offspring from less religious families in their local Whit Walk.

To this day, older relatives mutter darkly about lapses in parenting if the younger generation are not kitted out for this occasion, walk or no walk. This popular movable feast remained a holiday until 1971 when it finally lost its floaty status dependent on Easter and was replaced by the Spring Bank Holiday on the last Monday in May. Some walks still continue, accompanied as they ever were by brass bands, another strong northern tradition. Having flourished in tandem with the growth of industry, they began to decline as the industries themselves declined. However, one product of this fine tradition marched further afield into all sorts of corners of the world – and is still marching onwards as to war (join in if you know the words).

In 1865 a young curate by the name of Sabine Baring-Gould took a break from his study of were-wolves (yes, were-wolves) to dash off a hymn for the children's Whitsy Walk from his parish at Horbury Bridge to St Peter's Church near Wakefield. The lyrics had staying power, and gained further popularity when Arthur Sullivan (of Gilbert and Sullivan fame) wrote them a tune. The hymn, 'Onward, Christian Soldiers', has been marching ever since, not least as the Salvation Army's pet processional anthem for its mission as soldiers of Christ.

When Sir Winston Churchill met Roosevelt in 1941 to hammer out the Atlantic Charter, he chose this hymn to be sung at the service on board the battleship HMS *Prince of Wales*, explaining afterwards that 'we had the right to feel that we were serving a cause for the sake of which a trumpet has sounded from on high'. The militaristic associations of the hymn caused it a few problems in the 1980s when there was a campaign to have it struck out of the United Methodist Hymnal. However, the response from its fans, in congregations far and wide, saved it.

In contradiction of its military connotations, 'Onward, Christian Soldiers' went on to play its part in historic peaceful protests. Dr Martin Luther King Jnr and other civil rights campaigners in America saw the value of this hymn for expressing the idea of fighting a fight under the banner of peace. Not a bad record for a 15-minute bout of last-minute creativity, but the curate who wrote it was an unusually prolific fellow, producing more than 1,200 publications in his lifetime. His study of lycanthropy speaks for itself and *The Book of Were-wolves* became a definitive work in its own right. As for the hymn, 'crowns and thrones may perish, kingdoms rise and wane', but 'Onward, Christian Soldiers' has endured the march.

A WAGGLY ONE
1870

Yorkshire terriers were not recognised as a breed until 1870. They were developed from broken-haired Scotch terriers, a much larger breed, brought into the county by working-class Scotsmen who arrived in Yorkshire seeking work on weaving looms. It is believed they were selectively bred towards miniaturisation to help keep down rats in the booming mills.

These little dogs are very much terriers by nature, being spirited and socially engaging, and it is one of their number, Sylvia, who holds the world record for being the smallest dog ever recorded. Fully grown she measured two and a half inches to the shoulder, was a mighty three and a quarter inches long and weighed just four ounces. Bless her! She died at the age of two, which doesn't even add up to much when calculated in dog years.

It is not uncommon to hear gruff Yorkshire types expressing disapproval for diminutive canines, particularly the nervous ones, but the Yorkie with its plucky personality and rough-and-tumble capabilities seems to escape the customary taunts levelled locally at tea-cup breeds, such as 'that's not a dog – it's a rat' or 'get it on a stick and wash t'winders wi' it!'

One Yorkshire terrier in particular deserves a mention, having done much useful work in the field of international canine diplomacy on behalf of the Yorkies' right to call themselves proper dogs: Smoky. She was just seven inches tall and weighed four pounds, a giant in comparison to the above-mentioned Sylvia, but her strange life is regarded as a significant one in reviving the popularity of this breed.

Smoky was already fully grown when she was found during the Second World War in a foxhole in the New Guinea jungle. She was immediately sold on for the sum of two Australian pounds, the stake her finder needed for a poker game. Initially she was thought to belong to the Japanese and was tested with both Japanese and English commands, neither of which she understood. Filthy and emaciated on discovery, this doglet was to become a famous, decorated war dog and a pioneer of canine palliative care, giving cheer to the wounded in field hospitals. American GI Corporal William A. Wynne never regretted the two pounds he paid for Smoky, the Yorkie Doodle Dandy.

By the end of the war, she was credited with 12 combat missions in the South Pacific and had been awarded 8 battle stars as a member of the 5th Air Force, 26th Photo Recon Squadron. An unofficial war dog, she had none of the usual specially formulated rations, and survived by sharing Wynne's and sleeping in his tent. Smoky was never sick, neither did she develop the foot problems prevalent among working dogs in that area from running on coral. She learned a huge repertoire of tricks and had her own parachute, the use of which she demonstrated from the tops of trees. Smoky could even walk a tightrope wearing a blindfold. *Yank Down Under* magazine declared her 'Champion Mascot of the South Pacific Area', the fame of which allowed her to first enter field hospitals to perform for the wounded.

Smoky was decorated for her contribution to the war effort when her skills were requested to help with the building of an important Allied airbase at Lingayan Gulf, Luzon. The signal corps needed to run telegraph wires beneath the airfield, a dangerous and lengthy task for a construction detail, digging on the runway's exposed ground. Dangerous also for the 250 crewmen who would have had to keep the 40 resident US war and reconnaissance planes on the move so as to be operational while the runway was dug up. All those involved would have been put at serious risk from enemy fire if Smoky had not been there to help. She carried the end of the telegraph wire along 70 feet of narrow pipework under the airfield, digging her way through where the corrugated joints had allowed soil to leak in and form blockages. Even for one as small as Smoky there was little room to catch a clean breath of air. Thus, a risky three-day operation for several hundred men was completed in under ten minutes by the smallest, hairiest member of the team.

After the war Smoky went home with Wynne to his native Cleveland, Ohio, travelling aboard ship in a modified oxygen-mask box. She became a national sensation, making front-page stories and appearing in many TV shows. In 42 live TV appearances she never once repeated a trick. 'Corporal' Smoky and her comrade Wynne travelled all over the world, performing and talking about their experiences, but were most committed to brightening up veterans' hospitals, continuing the work Smoky had begun back in 1944 as the first ever recorded therapy dog, in the 233rd Station Hospital in New Guinea.

Smoky died suddenly in 1957, aged approximately fifteen. Buried by her family in a .30-calibre ammo box, she was given a posthumous award for service by the PDSA and the annual Yorkshire Terrier National Rescue Award in the United States carries her name, in honour of her own humble foxhole beginnings. Fifty years after her death, on Veterans' Day in 2005, a monument was erected over the final resting place of this little tyke: a large granite base supporting a bronze life-sized sculpture of Smoky sitting in a GI's helmet. The monument bears a dedication 'To Smoky, the Yorkie Doodle Dandy, and the Dogs of All Wars'. All 'four pounds of courage' as she was known, Smoky is there as a reminder – it's not the size of the dog in the fight, it's the size of the fight in the dog.

DOUBLE-OH SWALLOWS
AND AMAZONS
1884

Years before J.K. Rowling hit the literary charts and claimed the hearts of modern youth with her dual-reality wizard world in *Harry Potter*, generations of children were captivated by *Swallows and Amazons*. Set in a semi-recreated Lake District, honourable middle-class children enjoy camping adventures on Wildcat Island and sail their little boats with an attention to protocol to make their distant naval commander father proud. These are tales full of school holiday freshness and imagination, made real by detail: how to build a fire, how to communicate using semaphore, or the best way to scull and moor a dinghy. Their author, Arthur Ransome, the epitome of pipe-smoking English respectability, upholding pure and simple moral values, was certainly a spy, and almost certainly a double agent. In the throes of the Russian Revolution, he married Trotsky's personal secretary, while being known in the MI6 payroll department as agent S76.

Born in Leeds in 1884, the son of a Literature and History professor, he was educated at Rugby School, where he failed academically. He began work as an assistant in a publishing house in London, trying desperately to make it as an author. In 1909 he married Ivy Walker, with whom he never got on, and they had a daughter. They were miserable together for four years, part of which time was consumed by an unpleasant, high-profile libel case brought against Ransome for his biography of Oscar Wilde. When he finally won the case in 1913, he moved to Russia, ostensibly to research old folk tales, although his biographer, Roland Chambers, suggests that 'The Motherland' being one of the only countries at that time that required travellers to have a passport may have influenced his 'defection'. Neither his wife nor his daughter had one!

Arthur Ransome was something of a bohemian and his wide-eyed socialism fitted him well for Russia at that time. With the outbreak of the First World War, he stayed on there and became a correspondent for the *Daily News* and later the *Manchester Guardian*. He heard the speeches of the great Bolsheviks first-hand, was about the first British journalist to interview Trotsky, and wrote enthusiastic articles about the enormous political tidal wave that brought about the February and October revolutions. Ransome met the love of his life, Yevgenia Shelepina, as she sat typing and he sat waiting, in the anteroom to Trotsky's office. He knew Lenin personally, elaborated British foreign policy for the Cheka (the secret police organisation at that time), and actually shared an apartment with the Bolshevik propaganda chief, Karl Radek. He and Yevgenia also ran diamonds to other parts of Europe to provide funding for the Comintern (the international Communist organisation). Not surprisingly, he was arrested and interrogated for treason on a return visit to Britain, but he won over his investigators with his classic response when asked what his politics were. 'Fishing' seemed to cover it, and by the end of the war MI6 had recruited him to their staff, probably because he was such a likably talented 'angler' and so unusually closely connected with the movers and shakers of the phenomenal red revolution.

He and Yevgenia set up home in Tallin in 1919, after he was bizarrely instrumental in ending the Estonian counter-revolutionary War of Independence. He was on his way back to Moscow as correspondent for the *Guardian* when he was asked to deliver a peace proposal to the Russian side on behalf of the Estonian Foreign Minister. This he did, travelling on foot between the two warring fronts and later returning the same way with an acceptance.

This remarkable incident sheds light on the mystery of his suspected double-agent status, which has raised question after question since his death in 1967, as more and more historical documents become available. First, the shock of his MI6 agent status, then in later years, KGB documents that suggest all sorts of involvement on the Russian side. Readers tend to develop an image of an author and like to compartmentalise them along with their works; they found it hard to reconcile the two Ransomes. The truth is, Arthur Ransome was a complex man who got on with everybody, one of a dying breed from the former British Empire whose political passport was his honour, his personality, and his code of decency.

He married Yevgenia in 1924, and when they returned to England, they bought a farmhouse in the Lake District, a place Ransome had been taught to love by his late father. In 1929 he published the first of his tremendously successful *Swallows and Amazons* series. The children in the story are fascinated by a mysterious elderly man who has a houseboat full of exotic trophies of his travels. They recreate him as Captain Flint, a retired pirate, who is both their fond friend and their favourite foe. Looking at the photo of Ransome on the back of his books, with his bald head, twinkly eyes and Trotsky-cum-walrus whiskers, it is not so hard to accept the two personalities of the man: a spy from the most turbulent upheaval of our political times, and a storyteller evoking the innocence and wholesomeness of pre-political youthful adventures.

BRAM STOKER'S *DRACULA*
1896

Whitby is an ancient east coast seaport and fishing village, where the River Esk reaches the North Sea. It is a charming resort of quays piled with lobster pots and lined with stalls of fresh crab and mussels. On a fine day it is a beautiful place to wander the higgledy-piggledy, uppy-downy streets of cottages or to sit on the pier and defend your fish and chips from gulls.

It wouldn't be right for the county, though, if it didn't have its sinister side. Irish-born Abraham (Bram) Stoker stayed here at the Royal Hotel while writing what was to become the great Gothic horror classic *Dracula* and there is a plaque on the wall to prove it. When the weather gets wild, you can see how he might have been inspired to imagine the vampire's arrival. Looking out at the harbour and its dark cliffs with the ancient ruined abbey silhouetted on the top, Stoker conjured up the *Demeter*, a mighty Russian schooner driven by a ferocious storm to crash into the pier, its dead captain lashed to the wheel. A huge dog leapt from the ship onto English soil and that was how Count Dracula arrived. Former journalist Stoker wrote his famous work in an epistolary style, a convincing multi-genre collection of letters, articles, diary entries and ships' logs, which give a sort of collective feeling of reality through the sheer variety of witness accounts.

It's not a true story, of course, although if you visit Whitby at the time of one of its many Goth conventions, when dark-clad individuals with pallid faces and blacked-out eyes flit in and out of the many cobbled snickets of this old town, you still get a sense of it. I've never seen so many decommissioned hearses sporting parking tickets as on this seafront, where the Dracula Experience is alive and kicking and ghost walks at dusk do a roaring trade.

In a departure from the original work, film portrayals sometimes show the canine-toothed Count arriving in England by being washed ashore in a coffin, thus avoiding the irritating queues at passport control and jostling at luggage carousels one associates with jaunts abroad. Coffin travel is not yet available at Thomas Cook's, nor would it be very comfortable, but for some in Yorkshire it has been adopted in the past as a convenient mode of transport. One Thomas Shaw, for example, a ship's captain who turned 'outlaw' after the Anglo–Spanish 1604 Treaty of London put an official end to privateering, built a house in the remote village of Wainstalls high above Halifax using salty old ships' beams in 1608. Whenever he came home, he got round the inconvenience of having a pirate's price on his head by having the crew bring his ship in at Morecambe and unload him in a coffin marked with a warning that the occupant had died of the plague. He had a black slave, bought in Latin America, who supervised transportation of his coffin, dragging it with a pony over the hills to his home. Everyone gave Shaw's 'contagious corpse' a wide berth, which is more than can be said for the cramped one he must have had inside the coffin.

The original manuscript of Bram Stoker's *Dracula* was thought to have been lost, but it turned up in a barn in Pennsylvania in the 1980s. No one knows how or why it got there, but there it was: 540-odd pages of type with hundreds of corrections in the author's own hand and his signature at the bottom. Interestingly it was titled 'The Un-Dead' in that early incarnation and it is suggested that Stoker changed its name to Dracula at the last minute. In the first film version it was renamed *Nosferatu* (after failing to obtain the rights to the original story), but I suppose if you happen to bump into a vampire, his name will be the least of your worries.

THE LITTLE NIPPER
1897

American poet and analyst Ralph Waldo Emerson is often quoted as saying, 'Build a better mousetrap and the world will beat a path to your door.' Like many of the best quotations, this is not what he actually said, and it is not quite as unwieldy or as poetic as his original statement, which involved more examples and finished with 'you will find a broad hard-beaten road to his house, though it be in the woods', but its short form has become a standard metaphor for the might of innovation.

James Henry Atkinson was a West Yorkshire ironmonger who patented his mousetrap prototype in 1897, and it proved to be an effective, affordable combatant to household vermin. Given this, it's amazing that it took so long for the definitive snapper mousetrap to be invented, when, as any *Tom and Jerry* fan will know, the issue of the pesky *Mus musculus* has been a long-standing domestic struggle. Beatrix Potter did much fine work idealising mice into lovable waistcoat-wearing gentlefolk, but that doesn't alter the reality of their disease-rich incontinent ways, the catalogue of parasites they carry, or their ability to slip through gaps as small as six millimetres. Even with their mouse-size brains, they are adaptable and rapidly develop tolerances to the latest poisons.

Humans have always been devising traps, initially as a means of catching things to eat and later as a way of protecting cultivated food from things that want to eat it. Traps have developed from primitive holes in the ground, through all manner of contraptions of varying efficiency, but up until the late 1800s, no existing model was any kind of competition for a good old-fashioned lean and hungry cat.

The euphemistically named Little Nipper was an overnight success and has never been beaten. Its four simple parts – a pine base, wire fastening, spring trap and triggering device – make it a worthy standard for Emerson's 'invent a new mousetrap' test. This has come to mean creating the best possible device, one that cannot be improved upon. The Little Nipper has earned the title of being 'irreducibly complex' – there is no simpler way of making it, no device that works better, it is a truly finished product in an unfinished world.

More than a hundred years later, after computers have been invented and reduced from the size of a sports hall to that of a postage stamp with no limits yet set, the Nipper still holds its original snapping-speed record at 0.038 seconds, capable of dispatching a wee beastie faster than thought.

Some were a little cheesed off with Atkinson's success and suggested that his invention was less than squeaky clean due to the patent of a similar design in America by William Chauncey Hooker three years earlier in 1894. It is arguable that Atkinson could have gotten wind of this from somewhere, but as the Little Nipper remains the fastest and most successful snapper around, the competition can keep their traps shut! James Henry sold the patent to Procter Bros of Leeds (not to be confused with Proctor & Gamble) for the princely sum of £1,000 in 1913 and the company still make them today. The design retains more than 50 per cent of the British mousetrap market and around half of the international one as well.

Its success to date mirrors Agatha Christie's play of the same name. *The Mousetrap* holds the record for the longest initial run of any show in history. It opened in 1952 in London's West End and after a 50th anniversary in 2002 and nearly 25,000 performances, it is still running.

THE FRIENDSHIP BETWEEN A YORKSHIRE BIG-GAME HUNTER AND SOME VERY SMALL AFRICANS

1905–07

In the early 1900s, Edwardian society became fascinated by the idea of African savages. Available accounts encouraged images of primitive cannibals and massacres. James Jonathan Harrison, a big-game hunter and an East Yorkshire landowner, travelled extensively in Africa and filled his home, Brandesburton Hall, with the heads, tusks and skins of many exotic creatures. He'd practically killed one of everything apart from that Holy Grail of hunters, the elusive white rhino.

On his return from a trip to the Congo in the late 1890s, Harrison showed his photographs of pygmies to friends, who chided him for not bringing home a few human trophies. This he set out to do in 1905, though he would not be mounting any heads on his walls. Harrison's efforts to engage pygmies in visiting Britain are not to be confused with others of the time. There are records of attempted abductions of pygmies for display at such venues as the Paris Exhibition, but he himself had no such intention. He enlisted the help of Mongonga, an enthusiastic pygmy youth, fully grown at three feet six inches tall, to lead him to a tribe and encourage a small group to travel with him to Britain. Reluctant at first, they finally agreed and embarked on a journey filled with complications, as documented in Harrison's diaries. The group of six – including Chief Baruti – were native to the Ituri Rainforest. They travelled on donkeys happily enough until emerging from the forest canopy, whereupon they all collapsed and fell off, unaccustomed to the heat of shadeless sunlight. This turned out to be a fairly minor issue compared with the difficulties they encountered with British Imperial might trying to prevent the group from setting foot on English soil, but they finally made it.

The pygmies were billed to appear at the Hippodrome in London to massive crowds. They were advertised as curiosities, halfway between anthropoid apes and man; newspapers reported them as the missing link, the closest thing to monkeys in human form, and so on. They were presented on stage in a mock-up of their native environment, where they drummed and performed a traditional war dance. At this time, many acts were struggling to get bookings and the variety trade was in something of a slump, but the pygmies were seen by thronging crowds totalling more than 100,000 people in their first season. After promotion of the group as savages akin to apes in newspapers and theatre bills, many went along in the spirit of freak-show entertainment and were surprised to discover how 'human' they appeared. Reviewers marvelled at the pygmy women giggling like English girls and saying 'Goodnight' at the end of their performances; others declared the show worth seeing as an illustration of what a job 'civilising' the Africans was going to be.

The most interesting moments in history illustrate many facets of the times. The visit of Chief Baruti and the five others is just such an event. Jeffrey Green's illuminating book *Black Edwardians: Black People in Britain 1901–1914* carries a detailed analysis of the two years they spent in Britain in Chapter 6 and is well worth a read. He explains the political response of the Foreign Secretary Lord Lansdowne, who went to some considerable lengths (in cahoots with Lord Cromer, then Governor of Egypt) to try and prevent the pygmies from travelling to Britain at all. It had long been in the interests of missionaries and colonialists to sustain the idea that Africans were utterly degraded and barbaric. Green also points out the contradiction between the general view that these short Africans were dangerous sub-humans and their welcomed attendance at both Buckingham Palace and the Houses of Parliament, armed to the teeth with spears and bows and arrows.

One account of a royal garden party tells of a pygmy suddenly shouldering his bow and wiping out a passing rabbit with formidable skill to the delight of the guests. This was a fascinating illustration of the extent to which these 'savages' changed the perceptions of the newspaper reporters and crowds who came in closer contact with these very real personalities.

Most heart-warming of all is their sojourn in Harrison's native seat of Brandesburton in the East Riding. He took them home at the end of the season to winter there and, with a magnificent show of northern hospitality, arranged for a glasshouse to be built onto Brandesburton Hall in order to recreate as best he could the comfort of rainforest conditions for his guests. In this period of rest from theatre performances, being exhibited at zoos and being prodded and measured by scientists at the Natural History Museum, the pygmies, four men and two women, settled into village life.

They became well known and well liked in the neighbourhood. Often they were to be seen in their customary attire of animal skins, with the spears and other weapons they always carried, popping to the village shop, playing football with the local children or hanging out for hours on end at the blacksmith's forge making their arrowheads from discarded horseshoe nails. They made a lot of friends, attended weddings and were said to be keen jokers. It's no surprise that they were respected in Yorkshire as tough, clever little folk who gathered wild honey without flinching at bee stings, illustrating that ignorance and prejudice is harder to sustain where people mix closely and share a community.

In November 1907, the pygmies gave their last performance and donated the proceeds to the local hospital before setting off back to the Ituri Rainforest with their friend, James Jonathan Harrison. They had been seen by upwards of a million British people while on tour and such was the impact of their visit to Yorkshire that the local newspaper carried reports of their safe arrival home to the Congo, finally, in March 1908.

THE GREAT CONAN DOYLE, TAKEN IN BY A COUPLE OF YORKSHIRE KIDS

1917

Do you believe in fairies? Sir Arthur Conan Doyle, the literary genius behind the criminal mastermind Sherlock Holmes, did. He set out to prove their existence with the help of two young lassies near Bradford, who had a penchant for artistic and mystical photography that even the experts declared was genuine.

In 1917 two young cousins, Elsie Wright and Frances Griffiths, were thrown together for the summer holidays. Frances, aged 10, had just returned to England with her mother after a long sojourn in South Africa, and she and her 16-year-old cousin spent many happy hours playing by the beck in the garden of their Cottingley home. It reads like the beginning of a *Famous Five* story and, like generations of children before them, the young ladies were often in trouble by teatime for their muddy skirts and wet shoes. Elsie's father was a keen amateur photographer and the girls borrowed his camera one day, with spectacular results. On development of the plate, a picture materialised showing Frances nose to nose with a group of dancing fairies! Arthur Wright dismissed the photographs with an awareness of the artistic abilities of his daughter, and by the production of their second picture, this time with Elsie about to shake the hand of a gnome-like individual on the lawn, he became exasperated and refused to lend them the camera again.

Elsie's mother, on the other hand, believed they were real garden sprites and took the photographs to the Theosophical Society in Bradford. They were greeted with all sorts of enthusiasm and passed upwards until they reached the hands of leading member Edward Gardner, who was beside himself with excitement. He was not an idiot, however, and sent the photos and original glass plate to experts for confirmation of their authenticity. The response was positive, if guarded; the photos being declared as genuine representations of whatever was in front of the camera – not, however, as evidence of the existence of fairies, a possibility regarded as totally far-fetched in the laboratories of Kodak and Ilford. This was good enough for Gardner though, who wouldn't have been high up in his field without a firm resilience to sceptics, and with his promotion of the pictures, it wasn't long before fellow enthusiast Arthur Conan Doyle got involved.

When a letter from the literary crime giant arrived at the Wright household, the family were impressed and gave permission for the photos to be used alongside his article on fairies in the Christmas edition of *Strand Magazine*. It sold out in no time, and fairy frenzy became a hot topic. There were five photographs in total by this time, charmingly whimsical little winged ladies communing with their seemingly innocent photographers, and Conan Doyle asserted at the end of his article his hope that the 'recognition of their existence will jolt the material 20th-century mind out of its heavy ruts in the mud, and will make it admit that there is a glamour and mystery to life'. The response was certainly mixed. Some were taken in by this fanciful idea; others pointed out that the author's knowledge of children was somewhat lacking. Clairvoyants came to Cottingley and saw fairies everywhere, while the girls saw none at all – an illustration of the awkwardness attending the intrusion of adults into a child's game.

It wasn't until 1983, more than 60 years after the Cottingley fairies hit the headlines, that the girls finally confessed to faking the images, using cardboard-cutout drawings they had copied from a book. If any of their original critics were still alive by that point, they would have been gratified that their suspicions, awakened by the unusually elegant Parisian coiffures sported by the wee people, had been validated at last. Strangely though, even at a ripe old age, only a couple of years before both ladies were to go to their graves, Frances still insisted that the last photo, the most ethereal of the group, was genuine.

Conan Doyle's obsession with the spiritual world clearly superseded any remembrance he had of what it is to be young, when the world of imagination is real enough for great delight, especially when it fools adults into a welcome dose of long-lost childlike wonderment. Childhood is indeed a place where there has always been 'a glamour and mystery to life', and long may it stay that way.

THE OLD SWAN HOTEL –
COLONEL MUSTARD, IN THE
LIBRARY, WITH THE CANDLESTICK
1926

In December 1926, the Queen of Crime, Agatha Christie, an author whose sales are said to rank third in the world (topped only by the Bible and Shakespeare), suddenly and mysteriously disappeared from her Berkshire home after her husband admitted he was having an affair. Not long after the alarm had been raised her car was located, with its headlights on and bonnet up, near a lake in Surrey known as Silent Pool. It contained her fur, her clothes and an expired driving licence.

Amid wild speculations of suicide and abduction a massive manhunt was instigated, involving sniffer dogs, around 500 police officers and countless civilians. The lake was dredged and search aeroplanes were used for the first time. Given the status of the missing person, it is perhaps not surprising that great crime-writing contemporaries such as Sir Arthur Conan Doyle and Dorothy L. Sayers got involved in the search; in fact Conan Doyle's obsession with the occult led him to take one of Agatha's gloves to a medium in the hope of discovering some vital otherworldly clue.

Conan Doyle's Sherlock Holmes' mysteries were an early inspiration to Agatha Christie and encouraged her in the creation of her famously complex plots and much-loved eminent detectives. When she finally killed off her most popular character, Hercule Poirot, in *Curtain*, he became the first fictional character to have an obituary published in *The New York Times*, justified by his appearance in no fewer than 33 novels and 54 short stories. If she had killed him off sooner he might have been available to respond to Conan Doyle's medium and helped to shed some light on the increasingly baffling disappearance of his creator. The glove bore no fruit and neither did more official avenues of enquiry. The Queen of Crime had vanished.

It was the Old Swan Hotel in the Yorkshire spa town of Harrogate that provided the denouement for this 11-day mystery of proper whodunnit proportions. Prior to that, the building had had its own share of history. A pretty, ivy-clad, listed building, offering accommodation since 1777, it became a fashionable spa hotel in the nineteenth century, complete with Turkish baths for hydropathic therapy, and was renamed the Harrogate Hydro. It was the first building in Harrogate to have electric light, generated by the power of a vertical steam engine. In 1939 the hotel was requisitioned by the Ministry of Aircraft Production and it was attacked by an enemy plane in 1943. It survived, and was returned after the war to its former glory as a genteel hotel for gracious visitors taking the waters.

Back in 1926, one particular single lady, a supposedly recently bereaved Miss Theresa Neele from Cape Town, caught the eye of the Swan's banjo player, Bob Leeming. He recognised her and revealed her true identity to the police. Agatha Christie had checked in under this assumed name for the duration of the hunt and had had a gay old time at the elegant dinners and dances of Harrogate. The surname she had chosen for her concealment turned out to be that of the mistress her husband had confessed to on the night she vanished.

She never spoke of what happened in the missing 11 days, claiming complete memory loss, although it is generally assumed that she had a breakdown following the death of her mother earlier that year, made worse by her husband's declaration of his infidelity. Several biographies have explored what might have happened. Suggestions range from it being an elaborate hoax to put the willies up her erring spouse, to the possibility that she suffered from a syndrome by the name of 'dissociative fugue', which tends to present as a trauma-related departure on a journey, often accompanied by loss of memory.

Her husband, Colonel Christie, hastened to Harrogate as soon as she was found and, despite her making him wait in the lounge while she finished dressing for dinner, the couple remained together for two more years before finally calling it a day in 1928. Bob Leeming was given a beautiful silver cigarette case engraved with thanks from the Colonel and Mrs Christie. It was eventually sold for a hearty sum at Sotheby's by Leeming's descendants in 2012.

The strangest part of this tale for me remains the fact that a Yorkshire hotel actually employed a full-time banjo player, but I suppose the 1920s weren't just 'roaring', they were plucking good fun as well!

WHATEVER HAPPENED
TO AMY JOHNSON?
1930

There are many available accounts of this pilot's short life, and they all seem to begin with powerful adjectives and superlatives. As a writer it makes me feel like history should reserve a few special-occasion words, well polished on the top shelf, for reflecting the spirit of a girl like Amy Johnson. She was an innovation, iconic; she had a lovely smile. She died in a mysterious plane crash in 1941. Let the salient details of her life speak for themselves.

Born in 1903, Amy was the daughter of a Yorkshire kipper factory owner, John William Johnson, a self-made man and one of the thousands of prospectors who set out to find fortune in the sensational Klondike gold-rush era. She was an unusual girl and seems to have inherited this pioneer spirit. At the age of 12 she drove her father's motorbike around her home city of Hull. Then she took up trapeze, an early indication of her future head for heights. At just 18 she began an affair with a Swiss businessman that went on for seven years and left a huge legacy of correspondence. She attended university in Sheffield, at a time when higher education for women was only the territory of occasional aristocrats, and graduated with a BA in Economics.

Things became a bit strained when she finished her studies and went back to her parents' home. Amy was frustrated and in need of an outlet for her restless ambition so she moved to London, where the best she could manage was a job working as a shorthand typist, an appropriate situation for a highly qualified woman in the 1920s, sad to say, and one only procured through a quiet word from a family friend. Voting equality with men was not far around the corner but Amy couldn't wait, she simply had to find a way to make her mark. She had often admired the aerodrome at the London Flying Club through the bus window and one day, she got off there. After that seminal decision, every spare penny of her income was translated into flying lessons. Just a year later, in 1929, she not only gained her pilot's 'A' licence, she became the first woman to be awarded an Air Ministry Ground Engineer Licence. Amy had found her outlet.

A year later, with only 75 hours of flying experience to her name, she made history as the first woman ever to fly solo to Australia, a journey of about 10,000 miles. The furthest she had flown before that was from London to Hull, about 200. She had worked hard to find sponsorship, writing countless letters appealing unsuccessfully to anyone she could think of, but the people she managed to meet face-to-face bought into Amy Johnson. Lord Wakefield, head of Wakefield-Castrol Oil Company, agreed to share the cost of a plane with her father and, equally importantly, he arranged for fuel to be available at points along the route. The plane, a second-hand De Havilland Gypsy Moth which cost £600, was inadequate for such an undertaking as well as in need of repair. Amy repaired it, named it *Jason* (after the trademark of the family fish business – not the guy with the Argonauts), and in a couple of weeks she was ready to go. Hardly anyone saw her off, but by the time she reached her first stop, Karachi, she had become an international celebrity. She had also beaten Bert Hinkler's record for this journey by two whole days. She went on to complete her epic adventure, hampered by crash landings, maintenance trouble and bad weather, in 20 days. The crowds went wild.

Her return to Croydon was very different from her departure. Around a million people lined the route from the airport to central London. Amy Johnson, brave lass that she was, had captured the hearts of the nation and a CBE, presented by King George V. Her life changed dramatically as the gala-luncheon and glittering-soirée circuit took over. She became a fashion leader and a subject for popular songs.

The 1930s were ripe for a female figure like Amy Johnson. She certainly wasn't the only woman of the time making her way as a flier but she was from by far the most humble background, despite her father's wealth. Looking at footage of Amy, it is easy to see what made people love her: a handsome woman full of radiant energy and good cheer, who was forthright in speeches and equally fitted for elegant circles as she was for a hangar and spanners. She didn't forget her home town either. Using £25 in sovereigns, which had been presented to her by the children of Sydney, she commissioned a gold cup to be awarded annually for a single outstanding act of bravery by a Hull child. The Amy Johnson Cup for Courage, as it is inscribed, a bonny trophy with winged women for handles, is still awarded to this day.

Amy married the famous aviator James Mollison in 1932. She had met him in Australia after overshooting a runway and damaging *Jason*. Mollison had offered to fly her to her next engagement, which turned out to be more than one when he proposed in the air. Talk about a whirlwind romance; they had known each other for about eight hours all told. The fashion and society pages went *Hello*-magazine-style gaga over the couple, although in reality the marriage was a turbulent one. Mollison was a carouser and a womaniser, already accustomed to social attention and fame, and it didn't help that Amy broke all her husband's flying records nearly as fast as he set them. She destroyed his London to Capetown record by 11 hours. The couple divorced in 1938, from which point Amy is said to have tried to lead a quieter life outside the public eye. (This is contradicted by her competing in the Monte Carlo Rally in 1939, but this was only a brief foray into the world of automobiles.)

Determined as ever to maintain a career in aviation, she joined the Air Transport Auxiliary corps in 1940 to do her bit for the war, a job that would be her last. On 5 January 1941 Amy Johnson was killed on a seemingly routine mission to ferry an Airspeed Oxford plane from the production site in Blackpool to RAF Kidlington in Oxfordshire. She took off alone in thick, freezing fog. What happened to her after that no one knew, or no one was ready to admit. Four and a half hours later, what should have been a 90-mile journey across England ended as the plane plummeted into the Thames Estuary, 100 miles off its intended course. HMS *Haslemere* was in the area and hastened to assist. Amy called out to identify herself and was thrown a rope that she couldn't hold due to the extreme cold. The *Haslemere*'s captain, Lieutenant Commander Walter Fletcher, dived in to save her but failed. Amy's body was never recovered and the heroic captain died of hypothermia shortly after he was hauled back on deck. Sixty years later a former RAF clerk, Derek Roberts, admitted to having written up the report on her death given by eyewitnesses on board. The ship's engines had been thrown into reverse to stay alongside Amy, who it seems was tragically sucked under by the propellers and chopped to pieces. It is believed that this report was suppressed at the time as being bad for wartime morale. The military can't really be seen to go round accidentally dicing up its own national icons, although of course these things do happen.

The greater mystery contained in the report lies in eyewitness claims that there were two people in the water, not one. There has been much conjecture as to the identity of the enigmatic Mr X. Rumours of Amy being involved in transporting spies, politicians or even a German lover have been fuelled by the plane's being so wildly off course. Realists with knowledge of the problems involved in early aviation accept that bad weather and errors of judgement would be more than adequate as explanations for such a deviation. Biographer Midge Gillis is also sceptical about Mr X and suggests that the pigskin bag Amy had with her could have appeared like a head and shoulders in the water. The actual reason for the flight is still a government secret, so no official reports have ever been released to shed light. As with so many strange tales, the reader is left to make up his or her own mind. Amy could easily have been involved in special missions like her equally famous German counterpart Hannah Reitsch, who even popped in to Berlin as it was collapsing under Russian fire to say a personal goodbye to the Führer before he and Eva Braun killed themselves. Strange tales exist because strange things happen.

The diminutive *Jason* with his green paint and silver lettering now hangs high in the eaves of the Science Museum in London. He looks adorable, like an old kid's toy, and yet he reflects the golden age of flying and the achievements of a remarkably brave young woman.

A CAT, A CLIFF AND A
LIFE-SAVING INVENTION
1934

Late on a pitch-dark, foggy night in the Pennines, Percy Shaw was making his way home from his local pub, The Dolphin, in Clayton Heights, Halifax. He was driving down a winding road with a sheer cliff drop on one side and a solid stone wall on the other. The fog was thick as smoke and the headlights only served to light its swirling against the windscreen. Percy, like many other Yorkshire drivers abroad after last orders in those days, navigated with his sidelights, lining up one wheel with the tramlines and following their dim reflection. Legend has it that on a particularly sticky bend, he lost his line but was saved from the cliff edge by the emerald flash of a cat's eyes as it crouched on a fence and glared at the car. He righted himself and got home safely, with a brilliant idea for making roads safer.

In 1934, Percy Shaw, the son of a humble dye-house labourer and one of 15 children, patented his safety road stud and went into business. Consisting of two pairs of reflective crystal glass balls set into a vulcanised rubber casing, housed in cast iron, the Catseye, as they were trademarked, is squashed down when car tyres run over them and contains a well to catch rainwater so that the eye is washed as it winks. As Alan Whicker said when he interviewed Percy Shaw on his popular programme *Journey in a Lifetime* in the 1960s, 'Each one is a blinking marvel!'

Business was slow in the first couple of years, but Reflecting Roadstuds Ltd took off in earnest after the undeniable success of cat's eyes during the blackout of the Second World War. They were a tremendous asset to drivers with wartime shuttered headlights, which recreated for drivers all over the country the difficult conditions encountered as standard in the hazardous climate of rural Yorkshire. After the war, they were promoted by the Ministry of Transport and production rose to around a million units a year. It wasn't long before cat's eyes were in demand worldwide. Percy was given an OBE in 1965 and ever since the cat's eye has remained a standard feature of road safety everywhere.

Percy Shaw was the epitome of dour Yorkshire solidness. Humourless-looking to outsiders, he was a highly valued and entertaining companion to those who knew him, with a twinkle like one of his products in his unsmiling face. A businessman who could have made his healthy fortune significantly healthier had he allowed international franchises to make his product, he kept the patent exclusively at home in Halifax. This was said to be due to his distrust of foreigners, but Percy had travelled to Czechoslovakia, as it was then known, in order to secure the best crystal glass while perfecting his prototype invention. He lived his whole life (from the age of two, when his family moved there) in 'Boothtown Mansion', and the factory grew right next to it. Percy had his factory carefully built to incorporate the sycamore tree he liked to climb as a child. Not wanting to have it cut down, he insisted it should be allowed to continue its life through the middle of the roof, unscathed.

Percy lived a fairly spartan life. He never married and in later years, despite his great wealth, his house was bare of carpets and had curtainless windows. He explained that carpets were smelly things, and he didn't like people who fussed over a bit of dropped cigarette ash; curtains got dusty, and the views from his windows were lovely, especially in snow, and shouldn't be shut out. His only concessions to luxury were the three televisions he kept in a row, one for each channel, which were kept on silent but never turned off, and his beloved Rolls-Royce Phantom. Percy was a generous host, a great one for parties, and his echoey rooms were kept as full of friends as they were empty of soft furnishings. He remained unspoiled by his success and lived to the ripe old age of 86.

In 1999, a cat's eye became dislodged from its casing on the M3 motorway as a van drove over it and it shot through the windscreen of the car behind, instantly killing the passenger, well-known drum and bass DJ Valerie Olukemi Olusanya, known as 'Kemistry'. This singular and tragic accident was an exception to the otherwise glowing record of cat's eyes, whose friendly glitter on dark and lonely highways has saved countless numbers of lives across the globe, earning Percy Shaw's creation a high ranking in the list of greatest British inventions.

FENELLA,
THE HOLMFIRTH TIGRESS
1939

The Sumatran tiger (*Panthera tigris sumatrae*) is classified as a critically endangered species with an estimated population of no more than 600 individuals remaining in the wild. Its distribution and habitat ranges from lowland forest to mountain forest on the Indonesian island of Sumatra, and to the Pennine hills and sofa cushions of Holmfirth in West Yorkshire. It is one of the smaller subspecies of tiger, weighing in at about 220 to 310 pounds and measuring around 8 feet in length, which may be small for a tiger, but remains quite a formidable prospect for those 'here, kitty kitty' moments when strolling round a Yorkshire village.

This last somewhat unlikely habitat came about when the Overends, a family of travelling circus performers indigenous to Yorkshire, were touring South Africa in 1939 and were offered a pair of twin cubs to foster. One of the cubs became sick and died; the other, Fenella, became part of the family and travelled home with them to Britain at the outbreak of the Second World War. She spent her days at sea snuggled up in a travelling blanket with the rest of the family amid the deckchairs on the ship's breezy decks, and after an inevitable spell in quarantine Fenella settled down to life in the Pennines quite happily.

The village of Holmfirth, made famous in later years as the setting for the long-running television series *Last of the Summer Wine*, has its fair share of eccentric inhabitants and became a major tourist attraction after characters like Nora Batty with her wrinkled stockings and welly-wearing Compo hit the screen. Coachloads of visitors in the 1980s and 90s came to spot for themselves the many real-life counterparts of the stereotypical inhabitants portrayed in the series.

There was nothing stereotypically feline about former resident Fenella, though ... or was there? Recent efforts by local library staff have collected together many first-hand accounts from the older people of Holmfirth, who still remember the time when tigers roamed the area. One respondent, Jean Dyson, saw Fenella at Blackpool on her summer holidays. Another, Neil Smart, son of a local police sergeant from many years ago, recalled the tiger's habit of lolling on a tree branch and dropping down suddenly to make visitors jump. It's not hard to imagine the heart-stopping moments of surprise this must have caused, but it is fairly typical of playful feline behaviour, albeit on a rather larger scale than one might reasonably expect. Fenella was a cat, though a big one at that, and spent much of her time sleeping contentedly at home on the sofa. When out walking with the family she was happy to receive the strokes and tickles under the chin that are the acknowledged right of all local moggies, and she was adored by the children of the nearby Nabb primary school, who would hang over the playground walls to pet her at playtime. Since modern rulings on Health and Safety have gripped all old-fashioned fun firmly by the scruff of the neck, it is impossible to imagine the local authority risk assessment that would be needed to cover this sort of eventuality nowadays; a document longer than Fenella's tail with more clauses than she had claws, no doubt.

The story of the Holmfirth tigress highlights what has always been so special about rural village communities. They have a way of accepting and adapting to anyone or anything that somehow comes to belong, even if that something takes the form of a large, striped predator which could suddenly leap over a stile and confront anyone out for a country walk.

Fenella died in 1950 and was very much missed. She never hurt a soul and wasn't tempted to eat the neighbours, despite living through the period of wartime rationing, which she seems to have endured with as much dignity and restraint as anyone else.

THE YORKSHIRE ACCENT
COMBATS NAZI PROPAGANDA
1941

Halifax-born Wilfred Pickles made history in November 1941 when he read the midnight national news for the BBC Home Service. His was the first ever regional accent to be used in a BBC broadcast and he delighted Yorkshire listeners with his sign-off catchphrase '… and to all in the North, good neet.'

This may not seem like a significant event given the wealth of regional dialect that prevails in modern broadcasting; however, at the time of Mr Pickles' debut, traditional Received Pronunciation (RP), the neutral prestige accent of British English, was the alpha and omega of media presenting. Modern RP is simply an accentless English, whereas traditional RP is the ultra-posh pronunciation associated with 1950s public information films and older members of the royal family. When the BBC began in 1927, its founder Lord Reith designated traditional RP as the type of speech which would best be understood by the greatest majority of listeners. This is true in so far as it favoured no particular region, but of course as the vernacular of the aristocracy and top-flight public schools it encapsulated a small and privileged minority. Allowing Wilfred Pickles to penetrate this enclave with his flat vowels and unvoiced consonants broke the mould.

What could easily be mistaken as an attempt to give some representation to the common people was in fact a move to hamper Nazi propagandists, who had become adept at imitating the BBC's broadcasters and creating fake news reports using 'Lord Haw-Haw' announcers on radio programmes such as *Germany Calling*. The name Lord Haw-Haw was a generic term which eventually became more exclusively attributed to William Joyce, the most prominent of

Germany's English-language broadcasters. A senior member of the British Union of Fascists before the war, he fled to Germany in 1939 after receiving a tip-off that he was intended for internment. He was eventually captured in Germany by British forces towards the end of the war and was hanged for treason on 3 January 1946 by long-standing British executioner Albert Pierrepoint, a Yorkshireman with a chapter of his own, who turns out to have hanged more than one of the personalities mentioned in this book.

Joyce's broadcasts, along with those of others of his ilk, were orchestrated by the Reich Ministry of Public Enlightenment and Propaganda as a means of demoralising English-speaking troops. They devised false reports on the effectiveness of the Allies, and gave a high profile to massive casualties among the Allied forces and the sinking of Allied vessels. The BBC had tried various methods of reducing the risks of imitation before resorting to Wilfred Pickles. In 1940 they dispensed with their hitherto unbroken tradition of nameless newsreaders when Frank Philips identified himself on 13 July while reading the lunchtime news. It was a step in the right direction but it didn't really help, as presenters were so carefully collected from such a rarefied group that they all sounded very similar to each other and Lord Haw-Haw.

There was a mixed reaction to Pickles' first broadcast. He became a hero overnight for some listeners, some were outraged and some were even reported as doubting the veracity of the news when he was reading it. Nevertheless, this proud Yorkshireman quickly became a celebrity and went on to an acting career in West End theatre, in film and on television. The most notable of his films is the 1963 adaptation of Keith Waterhouse's play *Billy Liar*, in which Pickles plays alongside Tom Courtenay, Julie Christie and Leonard Rossiter as the father of the protagonist Billy Fisher. *Billy Liar*, which the British Film Institute named in its list of top 100 British films, is not only a wonderful monument to the 'Are-you-boppin'?' style of courting of the late 50s/early 60s ballrooms, it was filmed using real locations in Bradford prior to major redevelopment and contains some stunning historical footage of the city and its post-war atmosphere. A British New Wave film, it has a characteristic documentary feel and is radical in that Mona Washbourne, who plays Billy's mother, has the risqué task of uttering the swearword 'pissed', a first for commercial film standards of that time.

Pickles was also host of one of the most popular BBC radio shows ever, entitled *Have a Go*. This quiz show first aired a year after the war and ran for more than 20 years. He co-presented *Have a Go* with his wife Mabel, travelling up and down the country broadcasting from church halls, where local people were interviewed about their heart-warming everyday experiences. Pickles remains famous for his many catchphrases such as 'What's on the table, Mabel?' delivered in his inimitable style – that quite literally inimitable style – which was used to confound the Nazis. He was awarded the OBE for his services to broadcasting in 1950.

A VERY STRANGE EDITION OF THE YORKSHIRE POWST

1944

In 1944 the *Yorkshire Post* printed a very unusual edition. It had travelled a long way, passing in secret through fences, borders and checkpoints to arrive, already laid out properly for press, on the editor's desk. It had come from Stalag Luft VI, the northernmost of the Third Reich's POW camps. This remarkable work was produced, against all odds, by Yorkshire prisoners who were missing God's Own County. How it was achieved illuminates the resourcefulness of the soldiers: duty-bound as they were to seek opportunities to escape, these men managed at least to smuggle a part of their creative selves to freedom.

The *Yorkshire Post*, the county's broadsheet newspaper, celebrated its 250th anniversary in 2004. Something of an original for a local paper, it began as the four-page *Leedes Intelligencer* in 1754 and became the *Yorkshire Post* in 1866 when it was bought by a group of Conservative-supporting businessmen. The *Post* went from a weekly to a daily at this time and quickly gained a reputation as a serious paper, including coverage of news and events beyond the boundaries of Yorkshire.

The *Post* is still regarded as leaning towards the right in politics and speaks out in true Northern style, as shown by its stance on hot topics like the hunting ban, which it opposed fiercely. It was the first British paper to cover the abdication crisis and scandalous affair of Edward VIII and Mrs Wallis Simpson, after unguarded remarks by the Bishop of Bradford gave it the lead. There had been plenty of sensational press about this shocking romance in other countries while the British press had refrained from sticking it to the Royals; however, there is little space for elephants in the room where Yorkshire people are concerned.

Also in the 1930s, the *Yorkshire Post* was unwavering in its opposition to the idea of seeking to appease Nazi Germany. Its philosophy consolidated the *Post* as a national broadsheet rather than just a vessel for 'kitten-stuck-in-tree' style local news. Unlike most provincial papers, it is available throughout the United Kingdom, which justifies its slogan 'Yorkshire's National Newspaper', although to those Yorkshire people who believe the county to be more than qualified as an independent state, there may be a deeper interpretation. This traditional loyalty of Yorkshiremen to their county combined with the ethos of the *Post* to produce the very unusual MS1553 Kriegie edition in 1944.

Stalag Luft VI near Heydekrug, Memelland, in Lithuania, housed 9,000 Allied airmen by that time. The 'Kriegies' as they were called by their captors, a short form of the German *Kriegsgefangene* (prisoners of war), formed societies in the camp where members could unite with others from their country, or county in the case of 'The White Rose'. People don't need to be far from home to find comfort in being surrounded by their own dialect and shared history. Sergeant Richard Pape came up with the idea of creating the newspaper as a means of boosting morale among members of the White Rose Society in Stalag VI. His job in peacetime had been on the *Yorkshire Post*'s editorial team so he was perfectly familiar with the format required.

Even the simplest equipment for the task caused problems. Paper had to be scouted out and snaffled in random sheets from under the watchful eyes of guards. Both pens and paper were banned from the possessions of POWs to cut down the risk of them being used to create false documents for escape missions, probably not without good reason in Stalag VI, which contained (temporarily) among its notable prisoners George Grimson, noted serial escaper and escape line organiser. Still, the White Rose Society managed to secure enough paper to produce a final draft of their newspaper totalling 84 pages! They made their own pens by reworking the steel banding around Red Cross pencils into inkable nibs. Once they had the right equipment, the job began in earnest to produce news and poems which depicted their lives, illustrated by caricatures, cartoons and drawings of their environment. It took five weeks to complete.

The finished newspaper was bound into plywood covers and set off on its way to Britain in the charcoal burner of a German doctor's car. Towards the end of the war many cars were adapted to become 'dual-fuel' using this Australian invention. It was not aesthetically pleasing and it certainly wasn't aerodynamic – a great metal cylinder which looked like a builders' brazier mounted on the boot – but it could burn enough charcoal to produce gas to power a car when petrol could not be found. Petrol may have been rare, but surely German doctors with British sympathies were even rarer, and this one took a great personal risk in smuggling the Kriegie's newspaper out of the camp.

When released, the 'Kriegie Edition of the *Yorkshire Post*' as it came to be known, was very well received. It brought reassurance from far away and an often humorous insight into life in the Stalag camps. Sir Winston Churchill read and praised it, and it served as a reminder to local families that in some corner of a foreign field, Yorkshire was still going strong. The *Yorkshire Post* had 300 copies of the paper made into book form, one for each of the Yorkshiremen finally repatriated in 1945. All the names and addresses of those who contributed are printed in the back. Copies of this very special edition of the paper are hard to come by, but the Yorkshire Archaeological Society Archive has one in its 'Treasures' section, and it is well worth a look.

HOW A HALIFAX SERIAL KILLER HELPED END CAPITAL PUNISHMENT

1953

This is the strange tale of a horrible man from Halifax. A tall, gaunt, mild-mannered individual with a piercing gaze and a whisper of a voice, John Reginald Halliday Christie helped put an end to the death penalty in Britain, but not before he himself had, directly or indirectly, been responsible for the deaths of at least nine innocent people. He became infamous as the Strangler of Rillington Place, the house where he killed and concealed his victims. More than 50 years later, the Royal Mail still receives mail for Christie at Number 10 Rillington Place even though it was renamed Ruston Close the year after he was tried and executed, and subsequently pulled down in the 1970s. The area where it stood in Notting Hill's Ladbroke Grove carries no traces of the original scene of his grizzly deeds and yet is a common place of pilgrimage for those fascinated by serial killers.

Born in West Yorkshire, the sixth of seven children, he was dominated by his five sisters. Christie developed an early obsession with death, which he suggested began at the age of eight when he saw his maternal grandfather laid out in his coffin. He had been very much afraid of this man and described a huge wave of contentment at seeing him lifeless. The family home overlooked a graveyard. Here, Christie liked to play for hours and he sought out cracks in the tombstones through which to peer into the graves. His lifelong issues with impotence began when he and a group of fellow adolescents 'paired off' for exploration and he found himself with a much older girl, who ridiculed him publicly for his inability to perform. Already an odd and unpopular boy, he gained the nickname 'Can't-do-it-Christie' and his self-esteem sunk further.

He enlisted in the army in the First World War and was injured by mustard gas, to which he attributed his low, whispering voice. Christie married Ethel Simpson Waddington from Sheffield at Halifax Registry Office in 1920, but remained unable to perform sexually except with prostitutes, and spent much of his time involved in petty larceny. Christie and Ethel stayed together for four unhappy years and then separated; while he continued a life of crime, she went back to her relatives in Sheffield. He served several sentences for theft and violence but, unfortunately for Ethel, the couple were reconciled after Christie completed a sentence of six months' hard labour for robbing a priest in 1933. Her life would have been very different had they not been reunited and had they not moved to London to start afresh at an address that was to become the most notorious in England twenty years hence – Number 10 Rillington Place.

With the outbreak of the Second World War Christie enlisted in the War Reserve Police. They failed to check his criminal record and he was accepted, one of many police errors in the ensuing case of John Christie that would allow him to rape and murder women unchecked for a period of 10 years between 1943 and 53. Notting Hill at that time could not have been further from the desirable Hugh Grant and Julia Robertsian boutique rich quarter it is today. Rillington Place was more Fagin than Madonna in terms of its residents and accommodation was overoccupied and squalid. Number 10 was divided into flats, with the Christies living on the ground floor. Only two of the flats had kitchens and none had a toilet or a bathroom. Many houses in the area were in a state of ruin from the Blitz.

The Christies were good friends with their neighbours, Timothy and Beryl Evans, a young couple who had moved into the top floor with their baby Geraldine. Tim was illiterate, and well known for his elaborate delusions of grandeur concerning brothers with limousines and suchlike. He scraped together an income painting and decorating, barely enough to feed his small family. Then, at just 19 years of age, Beryl fell pregnant a second time. She decided upon an abortion, and then she disappeared, along with their daughter – and Tim left town. Some weeks later Timothy Evans was arrested on suspicion of murder. Rillington Place was searched and the bodies of his wife and child were found strangled in the wash-house out the back. Evans blamed Christie, who he said had been responsible for carrying out an abortion that had gone wrong. Police questioned Christie, who was outraged at the suggestion and whose wife backed him up. Christie's word, as a former Reserve Officer, was taken over the word of Evans, a well-known liar, and the latter was convicted. Christie wept openly in the courtroom when sentence was passed. Timothy Evans was sentenced to death and, despite his desperate assertions that Christie was the killer, he was hanged at Pentonville Prison in February 1950.

The investigation was seriously flawed, not only because prosecutors were prejudiced as to the characters of the two men, but police searching Rillington Place had also missed some staggering pieces of evidence that would have pointed to a far bigger picture, not least of which was a woman's femur used to prop up the sagging fence beside the wash-house, where Beryl and Geraldine Evans had been found. Children playing in the Blitz rubble just over the wall from Number 10 had found and handed in a female skull that same week. The police made no connection and the real killer, Christie, was left to continue. Not long after this, Inspector Leonard Trevellian, who would later be involved in the Rillington Place murders investigation, chased a thief from the nearby market into the house and caught him in the top-floor flat. He went to see Christie, who acted as landlord, to inform him of the arrest upstairs. In the course of this conversation, Trevellian made reference to the rotten stink of the place, which Christie explained was due to those 'damned tenants'. It later turned out to be the smell of his decaying wife, poor Ethel Christie, who he had strangled and concealed under the floorboards.

It seems that many were taken in by Christie's calm and reassuring manner. As he buried his first victim – Ruth Fuerst – in the garden, he smiled and greeted passers-by, who reasonably assumed that he was just a pleasant fellow doing a spot of gardening.

The full horror of Christie's exploits as a serial killer came to light in 1953. He had moved out by this point and a new tenant, Beresford Brown, had taken up residence. Mr Brown was trying to put up a shelf in the kitchen for his radio when he realised the wall was hollow.

He peeled back the wallpaper, found a concealed door to an alcove and opened it. There he found the bodies of three young women, intact due to the winter cold, and the ensuing investigation of house and garden uncovered more – seven women in total. All had been strangled and sexually assaulted by Christie, who was recognised and caught by police near Putney Bridge a few days later. He never made clear whether he had raped his victims before or after death, but spoke at length of an overwhelming sense of peace and wellbeing that came to him each time he'd completed the process. He was tried and convicted, and hanged on 15 July 1953 by fellow Yorkshireman Albert Pierrepoint. Once his hands were bound for the execution, Christie complained that his nose itched. Pierrepoint consoled him with the words, 'It won't bother you for long.'

Richard Attenborough starred as Christie in the 1971 crime thriller *10 Rillington Place*, which was shot in the derelict Number 7. Based on Ludovic Kennedy's book of the same title, it explores the issue of Timothy Evans being framed by his neighbour for the murders of his wife and child. Evans had not lived at Rillington Place long enough to have been responsible for the murders of those women buried in the garden. Nor could he have been blamed for the ones after his death. The likelihood of two separate stranglers living at one address was so remote that the case against Timothy Evans was reassessed in 1966 and he eventually received a posthumous pardon from the Crown, which allowed his family to have him reburied outside the prison walls of Pentonville.

The case came to be known as a major miscarriage of justice and was strongly instrumental in the argument for the abolition of capital punishment. The Murder (Abolition of the Death Penalty) Act of 1965 suspended capital punishment for killing and was made permanent in 1969. Too late for Timothy Evans. Strangely, it wasn't until much later, in 1998, that the death penalties for treason and piracy were voted into obsolescence.

SEVEN MILES, SEVEN YEARS AND SEVEN MILLION POUNDS – BUILDING BRITAIN'S HIGHEST MOTORWAY

1963

> 'In winter the frost is always there before it comes to us; and deep into summer I have found snow under that black hollow on the north-east side!'
>
> *Nelly Dean, Wuthering Heights (Emily Bronte)*

Approaching Yorkshire from the west along the M62 motorway, the ground begins to rise steeply and green fields are replaced with the hills and heather of the Pennines. Bleak is beautiful around here, that wildness and turbulence of West Yorkshire at this altitude upon which Emily Brontë based her characters in a book that shocked the genteel literati of more easily civilised areas. As Mr Lockwood, the opening narrator of *Wuthering Heights*, and a southerner, explains, '..."wuthering" [is] a significant provincial adjective, descriptive of the atmospheric tumult to which its station is exposed in stormy weather'. Suffice to say that in 1963 when the M62 construction plan was given the go-ahead, civil engineer Geoffrey Hunter and his team were in for some serious atmospheric tumult as they began work on a seven-mile stretch of motorway that remains the highest in the country. Seven years of tumult, to be precise.

In 1949 the Special Roads Act was passed in Great Britain, allowing roads to be built specifically for a limited classification of vehicles, paving the way, if you'll pardon the pun, for the advent of trunk-road travel in the UK. Ten years later, the first section of Britain's first full-length motorway, the M1, was completed and inaugurated under its original title 'The London-Yorkshire Motorway'.

Motorways were not a local invention, the earliest having been built under Benito Mussolini's orders in 1920s Italy. These dictatorial beginnings continued as Germany opened its first Autobahn in 1931, followed by a national scheme notably developed by Adolf Hitler and the Nazis.

In the UK there was increasing demand for a sustainable transport route between Liverpool and Hull that would link in the huge industrial sites of Yorkshire and Lancashire. The A62, the original packhorse track along which strings of sturdy ponies laden with cloth bound for the port of Liverpool were led in days gone by, was hitherto the only route across the Pennines. Particularly in the harsh winters of the early 1960s when covered with up to 12 feet of snow, often for months on end, the A62 was fit for little else. Irrespective of their superior horsepower, lorries were constantly getting stuck and being abandoned until the thaw.

Something had to be done to tame a route as close to mountainous as one can get in British terms, and 28-year-old Geoffrey Hunter was given the challenge of creating a road that would remain open all year round. Hunter became something of a celebrity; a bright and enthusiastic fellow, he featured in much of the documentary footage for this project, which became a major tourist attraction in the mid to late 60s.

It's fair to say he earned it. Working at a height of 1,200 feet above sea level on a site that was mainly a peat bog, with winds of up to 110mph, he had to contend with sudden dramatic drops in temperature and out-of-nowhere fogs caused by settling clouds that blinded progress, sometimes for days on end. Hunter came to know a phenomenon long familiar to the indigenous population, that of rain forced *uphill* by high winds, which rains up the trouser legs as much as it rains down the jacket neck. A whopping 11.75 million cubic yards of peat surface had first to be removed from the site and deposited elsewhere on the hills. Vehicles had to be found that would not just sink into it. Cuttings needed to be blasted and 7 million cubic yards of rock had to be excavated to make Scammonden Dam, which was needed to hold a 200-foot-high motorway embankment.

The work schedule was set from 8 a.m. to 8 p.m., seven days a week, and coachloads of sightseers thronged the hillside on Sunday afternoons to watch the fun. As the reality of the grim weather conditions became clear, floodlighting was used and the schedule extended to 24 hours a day whenever conditions allowed them to work at all.

Objections were raised about the route cutting across the popular Pennine Way walk, and a special footbridge had to be built to keep it clear. Having dynamited Dean Hill Cutting, the largest single-span suspension bridge in Europe had to be constructed to accommodate the original B road. Seventy miles of scaffolding sustained this project, capable of holding the weight of 1,100 tons of ice. In the BBC documentary, *The Secret Life of the Motorway*, Hunter appears almost despairing in a cheerful sort of way at people's inability to appreciate the sheer scale of this bridge, pointing out that it is simply dwarfed in perception by the might of the landscape that contains it. In actual fact, Wembley Stadium would fit snugly beneath this average-looking construction. In later years it seems its loftiness has only been appreciated by those who no longer appreciate their own lives and it has become the area's most popular leap for suicides, taking advantage of the 100 per cent success rating at this location – if success is the appropriate word for such an accomplishment.

Perhaps the strangest part of this project is the eighteenth century Stott Hall Farm, which sits between junctions 22 and 23. Myths abound regarding this lone farmhouse. The motorway suddenly splits and is diverted – despite all that modern, energetic rock dynamiting intending to outdo the Romans in crow-flight terms – and the old white farmhouse sits firmly between the carriageways as if the six lanes of traffic don't exist for the occupants at all. They live on a deserted hilltop, much as they always did. This farm has become a symbol of Yorkshire people and their intransigence. It causes travellers to wonder at the fight that farm must have undertaken, and won. I have several times heard tell of a rural doctor back in the day before motorways were a twinkle in the transport minister's eye, when we had 'proper winters' and the locals made their way home along the tops of dry-stone walls barely visible between drifts. He had apparently attended a birth at this farmhouse and was met at the door by the old grandmother, who had suffered a gangrene infection in her foot many years before. Instead of getting outside medical assistance on that occasion, the family was said to have cut away her flesh to the knee so as to prevent the infection from spreading. The stump she walked around on into her old age was her own leg bone.

I, along with others hearing this tale, imagined that in comparison to this home remedy, seeing off a weighty government Compulsory Purchase Order would have been a fairly tame challenge. The reality is rather disappointing. The land upon which the farm stands was judged not geologically sound enough to support the motorway and the Wild family, then in residence, were not forced to sell up when others in the path of progress were. Still, as with the legend of Robin Hood, there is more in the perpetuation of the myth than the reality itself requires, and Stott Hall Farm is listed as one of the ten best-known sights from the motorway network, revered as a monument to defending one's home from the advance of the modern world. Its remote location has earned it the nickname, 'the Little House on the Prairie', initially between wagon drivers on CB radio and later extending to BBC radio traffic reports. It says enough about the Yorkshire spirit that everyone passing assumes the legend for themselves. That's a lot of legend given the average traffic flow for this stretch of motorway currently stands at between 70,000 and 100,000 vehicles a day.

Geoffrey Hunter and his team finally won their battle with the elements and the official opening at Scammonden Dam was performed on 14 October 1971 by Her Majesty the Queen, sporting an astonishing woollen hat with Dick Bruna-style daisies knitted into its pattern. Not a bad choice for the altitude though, and festive enough to mark such a major civil engineering achievement. The motorway does what it was intended to do and on days when it is not choking to death on its own traffic, the seven-mile stretch which cost seven million pounds and took seven years to complete can be traversed in just seven minutes.

TWO ALIEN OCCURRENCES IN TODMORDEN

1980

The village of Todmorden is an unusual place. Nowadays it sits on the border of Lancashire and Yorkshire and is somewhat impractically split. Half the town hall is in one county and half in the other. The cricket pitch lies in such a way that the bowler is in one county and the batsman another, creating a potentially sticky wicket. The ley lines are reputed to be strong in terms of alien and supernatural activity. Ghosts abound, and as in neighbouring Hebden Bridge, many settlers arrived here at the end of the Hippy Trail and set up home in the once shockingly inexpensive weavers' cottages. Witches live happily here, alongside what Joanne Rowling would term 'the muggle community', and an initiative called Incredible Edible Todmorden means that any and every bit of scrubland and bus-shelter side has corncobs and oregano winding up it. The greatest incidence of UFO and strange-light sightings in Britain occurs around the tall hills of Todmorden, in direct proportion – some cynics might say – to its having the country's finest upland conditions for the natural flourishing of psilocybin fungi, or magic mushrooms as they are more commonly known, due to their hallucinogenic properties.

The early 80s saw a major upsurge in reports of UFO sightings around this area and two very strange and vaguely connected events hit the national and international headlines. At half past three on 6 June 1980 Mr Zigmund Adamski, a 56-year-old coal miner, disappeared from his home in Tingley after nipping to the shop to get some potatoes. He was neither seen nor heard of for more than five days until his body was discovered on top of a heap of coal in Tomlin's Yard, Todmorden, on the afternoon of 11 June. The yard had been in use that morning, then locked up. There was no evidence of climbing on the coal heap, no coal on Mr Adamski's clothes, he simply lay face up on the top, having apparently suffered a heart attack. It was determined that he had been dead for eight hours. No one had seen him in the vicinity. Police officer Alan Godfrey attended the scene and discovered further peculiar details. Though Mr Adamski's clothes were tidy, his shirt was missing and his jacket buttons had not been done up to the corresponding buttonholes. His shoes had the appearance of having been put on by someone else and on closer inspection strange marks were found on the body, including burns to the back of the head and neck. Stranger still, some sort of gel-like substance had been applied to the burns two days previously, perhaps as an ointment, and forensic scientists failed to ever identify what the ointment was. It remained a mystery even after extensive research, which resulted in the death not being registered until the autumn. It has never been solved despite various investigations both by detectives and BUFORA, the British UFO Research Association, who were drawn to the scene. Curiously (although probably irrelevantly), a George Adamski, a Polish-American abductee, had become the first well-known claimant of interactions with alien life forms in the 1950s, although that appears to be the full extent of his connection to Zigmund. No answers ever emerged; however, that same year another incident from extra-terrestrial Todmorden hit the headlines.

PC Alan Godfrey, that same officer who had attended the scene of Adamski's death, was a well-respected and upstanding member of the West Yorkshire police force, twice commended for his investigation work, until his own strange experience cast doubt upon him. On 29 November 1980, PC Godfrey was sent to investigate repeated complaints from a Todmorden council estate that a herd of cows kept turning up in unlikely parts of their neighbourhood. This is not in itself an unusual case for a rural area, but this particular case changed Godfrey's life for ever. As he proceeded towards Todmorden on the Burnley Road, he saw lights up ahead that he took to be a stranded double-decker bus. When he got nearer, he reports that it was a strange, rotating, flying object floating five feet above the ground, full of energy but completely silent. Leaves swirled beneath it and the roadside foliage was affected by its breeze. He tried to radio through what he was observing but neither the car's VHF radio nor his personal UHF radio would work. Showing the sort of initiative that had probably earned him his previous commendations, Godfrey took out his notebook and began to sketch the object, noting what appeared to be a line of windows around its upper girth. He heard a very clear voice in his head and was unsure as to whether it was himself thinking or someone speaking. It said, 'You should not be seeing this. This is not for your eyes.' He then suddenly found himself in his car just past the sight of the incident and heading away from it. On looking at his watch, he reports that 15 lost minutes had elapsed. He had no recollection whatsoever of what had occurred in the missing quarter of an hour but one of his boots had a cut across the bottom of it as if he had been forcibly dragged and it had caught on something.

PC Godfrey didn't report this incident immediately as he felt it defied reality, and he went on his way to seek the roaming cows. Then, over the next few hours, as reports of strange-light sightings from other officers in the area began to come in, he felt he should add his own. One member of the public, a local school caretaker, reported seeing a bright light descending towards Burnley Road at the corresponding time, and three other policemen searching the neighbouring hills for stolen motorcycles reported seeing a large blue-white light hovering in that area. Godfrey and another officer returned to the scene, observing that although it had been a wet night (nothing strange about that in Yorkshire), the section of road where The Thing had allegedly hovered was completely dry. Strange indeed. Somehow the report was leaked to the press and a media field-day was had at the expense of the serious-minded PC Godfrey, beginning with a front-page story in the local paper entitled 'MAY THE FORCE BE WITH YOU!'

Godfrey could not deny what he had witnessed and MUFORA, the Manchester branch of the UFO association, again made their way to West Yorkshire. Under hypnosis, he described being removed to the interior of the craft and being telepathically addressed by a smiling humanoid individual on board. There was carpet on the floor inside, and machinery which caused him pain when he tried to look at it. The humanoid individual was accompanied by smaller horrible creatures with lampshades for heads (or lamp-like covers over their heads). They attached some sort of bracelets to his arms and legs, and two of the smaller creatures plugged themselves into the bracelets.

PC Godfrey became an important case for research, partly due to his very rational manner. He comes across in interview as a perfectly sensible man and his narration of events is consistent. Even after hearing recordings of himself being hypnotically regressed, he maintains that it was a mystery to him and that he accepted what he said might have been created in his subconscious from something he had read, dreamed or seen. A remarkable detail of the story involves a previous incident in 1973 when PC Godfrey had tried to arrest three wanted men who resisted. He was badly beaten, to such an extent that he lost a testicle and was told by doctors that his injuries would mean that he could no longer have children. Seven years later, immediately after his supposed abduction, he fathered a son.

Sadly, this incident did not augur continuing success in his career as a police officer. The once-respected PC Godfrey became something of an embarrassment to the force, it seems, and he was gradually made less and less a welcome part of the team. When his squad car was taken away and a bicycle offered in its place, PC Godfrey gave in and took early retirement. Like the Adamski case, no conclusions were ever drawn as to what caused these strange events, although there are suggestions that Godfrey had actually witnessed a UAP, or Unidentified Atmospheric Phenomenon, such as a fireball. Others suggest he experienced an ASC, or Altered State of Consciousness, after a long night shift. Whichever three-letter acronym seems most likely, it remains interesting that this area of Yorkshire towards the Lancashire border has been nicknamed UFO Alley on account of the high number of sightings reported. Between 1947 and 2001, 10,278 UFO sightings were logged nationally. Inhabitants of this scantily populated rural area are 12 times more likely to experience sightings than anyone elsewhere in Britain, and 73 per cent of all Pennine sightings have occurred within a 12-mile radius of Todmorden. There must be an explanation.

For those readers who like some sort of an ending to a strange tale, the best I can offer is that the lost herd of cows were eventually located. They were grazing peacefully in a locked recreation field accessible only by a small footbridge over a river. There were no hoofprints in the wet ground anywhere around the site. It was as if they had been dropped in the centre of the rugby pitch. How they got there is yet another mystery, and as none of the cows underwent hypnotic regressive therapy, we will never know.

THE YORKSHIRE RIPPER FINALLY CAUGHT

1981

The salient facts of Peter Sutcliffe's crimes are all too familiar to most. Targeting prostitutes, he brutally murdered and defiled 13 women and attempted to take the lives of seven others. His modus operandi – a swift blow to the head with a hammer, repeated stabbing in the throat, chest and abdomen with tools such as specially sharpened screwdrivers, followed by postmortem mutilations – allowed police to connect up the murders fairly quickly, despite their being spread over a wide area. However, the sheer scale of the enquiry and the lack of technology capable of processing the tons of data, added to the red herring of an elaborate hoaxer, caused huge problems in solving the crimes. Many a young police officer paid off his mortgage with the overtime this case created, and yet it was more or less by accident that Sutcliffe was eventually caught.

Initially, the general public were not especially concerned about the threat the Ripper presented because he targeted prostitutes. 'Decent folk' regarded themselves as safely outside the Ripper's remit until the fifth murder early in 1977 – that of 16-year-old Jayne MacDonald, his youngest victim and the first one not to be a prostitute. This widened the danger and redoubled pressure on West Yorkshire Police for an arrest.

In some ways, it could be argued that Assistant Chief Constable George Oldfield, the superintendent of the massive investigation for most of its duration, was Sutcliffe's 14th victim. His health and wellbeing were seriously affected by this case, which he was desperate to solve. He suffered a heart attack, was made to take leave and, though he subsequently returned to the task, he was ultimately removed from the case in 1980, a year before the arrest.

Oldfield became convinced that he had developed some sort of relationship with the killer, compounded by the hoax letters and a tape of a man with a Wearside accent he felt sure were real, which caused him to send the investigation off course for long enough to allow two more murders.

When Peter Sutcliffe, who closely resembled the numerous photofits, was finally caught, it became apparent that he had been interviewed a staggering nine times by police during the course of the enquiry. Many questions were raised over the effectiveness of the investigation, but the Ripper Squad had worked very hard and it was not for lack of trying that it took six years to catch the killer.

The enquiry generated so much information, all of which had to be processed and put into a card-index system, that it was impossible to manage. The floor of the incident room had to be reinforced just to support the weight of the paperwork involved. It is hard to imagine, now that computers have become a part of everyday life, just how unwieldy the case was. The last time Sutcliffe was interviewed at home, by Detective Constables Laptew and Greenwood, they felt sure they had their man. However, their report was lost, along with everything else in the drifts of documents awaiting filing, and did not surface again until after the chance arrest of Sutcliffe in Sheffield, which led to his confession. The two detective constables were frustrated by their report being dismissed to the pile, just because Peter Sutcliffe did not have the 'Geordie' accent recorded on the hoax tape.

On 1 October 1977, Sutcliffe murdered Manchester prostitute Jean Jordan. She was his sixth victim. Her body was found by allotment workers 10 days later and it was clear that the murderer had returned in the interim and further mutilated the poor woman's body. A hacksaw, which was later found along with a whole range of grizzly, modified tools at Sutcliffe's home in Bradford, had been used to try and decapitate the corpse, and other evidence of abuse suggested to investigators that the murderer had returned to remove something incriminating, had not managed to find it, and had taken his anger out on the body.

A further search of the area turned up the victim's handbag under some bushes. It was empty, but a side-pocket on the outside contained a brand-new five-pound note. This was a valuable piece of evidence, traced back via the Bank of England to a Midland Bank sub-branch in Shipley. It was part of a batch of 127,500 notes that had been distributed to more than 30 firms in the area for inclusion in the Friday pay packets. This meant that one of around 8,000 men had been given it the day before Jean Jordan's murder. Although the chances of the killer being the one who had received it were remote, 30 policemen were assigned to investigate and they interviewed more than 5,000 workers at local firms. They were demoralised by the enormity of the task, and the awareness that they could have interviewed the killer already. In fact he was interviewed twice, by different officers, in early November, but he and his wife had a strong alibi, a house-warming party, and this was further confirmed by Sutcliffe's mother, Kathleen.

Two years later, with an ever-increasing need to catch this monstrous killer, police returned to the five-pound note problem. They used an ingenious method to reduce the number of possible recipients from 8,000 to 300, by getting the original bank staff to re-enact counting out the money with dummy notes, reprinted in the exact sequence of those that included the ill-fated 'AW51 121565' fiver. This rather splendid piece of detective work should have done the trick. They had other clues to help them by this point, including a picture of the Ripper's bootprint, found once on the thigh of Emily Jackson in 1976, and on the bed sheet next to the body of Patricia Atkinson in 1977, and again very recently, beside Josephine Whitaker in 1979. Tragically, this phase of the investigation was damaged by the hoax material and George Oldfield's conviction that the letters and tape were indeed from the killer. Peter Sutcliffe was interviewed three times as one of the 300 possibles. He was asked to submit a sample of his handwriting, which of course didn't match the letters, and even though at one of these interviews he was actually wearing the boots that matched the footprint, he was again dismissed from the suspect list.

With hindsight it seems ridiculous that so much emphasis was laid on the 'Wearside Jack' hoax. None of the women who survived to describe their attacker ever said he'd had a Geordie accent, and none of the details in the letters were things only the killer could have known. A saliva test had been carried out on the envelopes and showed that the writer had type B blood, a group possessed by no more than 6 per cent of the male population, and the same type found in forensic evidence on the Ripper's victims, but 6 per cent still constitutes a lot of people. The tape should have been used as a line of enquiry rather than as a point of elimination. It was an emotional response from Oldfield in a high-pressure situation. The man responsible for the hoax, John Humble, was found nearly 25 years later through DNA testing in 2005, convicted of perverting the course of justice in 2006, and sentenced to 8 years' imprisonment. George Oldfield never recovered from the humiliation of the hoax; he took early retirement in 1983 and died two years later.

The officers who finally arrested Peter Sutcliffe had no idea they were bringing the most expensive enquiry in the history of the police force to an end. They had approached the car, which was parked down a track in Broomhill, Sheffield, because of the likelihood that the young woman inside, 24-year-old Olivia Reivers, was a prostitute. Sutcliffe said she was his girlfriend, but didn't know her name, and police suspicions were further roused by the car number plates, which had been stuck on with tape and didn't match the vehicle. Sutcliffe demanded to relieve himself and stashed the tools he was planning to use on Olivia in the bushes. After being driven to Dewsbury police station he hid another knife in the toilet cistern. Both were found the next day by officers following hunches. After two days of questioning he finally confessed, taking another day to explain details of his many murders. He was perfectly calm and civil, only later saying that God had told him to do it. Sutcliffe was granted permission to tell his wife that he was the Yorkshire Ripper. When charged, he was asked to remove his clothing, when further chilling evidence of his systematic approach came to light. Beneath his trousers, he was wearing a customised V-neck sweater. The arms formed leggings; the V left his genitals exposed for the convenience of sexual exploitation; there were hand-sewn pockets to conceal extra tools and the knee-areas had been padded for comfort.

Sutcliffe pleaded not guilty to murder, but guilty to manslaughter. His defence rested on his being 'the tool of God's will'. He claimed that he had heard the voice of the Almighty coming from the gravestone of a Polish man called Bronislaw Zapolski, when he had worked as a gravedigger in his late teens. His 30-year prison sentence was extended to a full-life tariff in 2010, so he will remain in captivity until his death. He resides in Broadmoor high-security psychiatric hospital under his mother's maiden name of Coonan. Sutcliffe has been attacked numerous times by inmates, leaving him scarred, blind in one eye and only partially sighted in the other.

THE YORKSHIRE BANK PLC
1982

In 1982 the Yorkshire Bank became the Yorkshire Bank PLC, marking the demise of its original and rather lovely history (for a bank), and it deserves a little elegy at least. We all hate banks, don't we? They are villainous, unfeeling places, full of suits and percentages, and the more moved we are by fiscal suffering, the less moved they seem to be. But the Yorkshire Bank was a bit different, worthy of the county it was named for.

It was founded by Lieutenant Colonel Edward Akroyd on 1 May 1859 in Halifax, a town that has become much more associated with its eponymous building society. Akroyd was a good man, rich as Croesus through an inheritance, which was then very much enhanced by his excellent skills in business. Mill owners of the time were not exactly first pick as philanthropists, tending more to contribute to the plight of their workers rather than to alleviate it, but Edward Akroyd felt things keenly and was genuinely concerned about horrific social conditions endured by the poor of Halifax, brought about as they were by the Industrial Revolution that had allowed Akroyd and his ilk to prosper. He ploughed his wealth (or at least some of it) into all sorts of schemes and institutions to improve the abject lives of the working classes: a school for child labourers, pension schemes, a local allotment society, and the first Working Men's College to exist outside London. It is perhaps a mark of his very thorough approach to a project that he built several churches and a cemetery as well!

The Yorkshire Penny Bank did what it said on the tin, and encouraged workers to save by offering them the chance to open a bank account with a single penny. It was a non-profit organisation and yet within the next two years it had opened a further 128 branches. There were sub-branches in church halls and they started the first school banks for children's savings. Altogether, it really wasn't half bad for a bank, and did its founder proud. People felt gratitude towards Akroyd and, when he died in 1887, his funeral at the lofty All Soul's church, a building he himself had commissioned and paid for, was attended by thousands of people.

The bank lost its Penny and became the Yorkshire Bank in 1959, and bloomed on until it was made a PLC. This had no immediate effect on the traditional values of the bank; when the Miners' Strike began in 1984, it gave deferment to miners who held mortgages there until such time as the strike finished and they might be able to pay. By 1990, though, it was owned by a consortium of banks from NatWest to Barclays and they sold it, lock, stock and barrel, to the National Australia Bank for a nice, tidy billion. Personally I'd like to think that the people who handle our hard-earned cash had a bit more of a sense of finesse for figures – it can't have been worth exactly a billion. Anyway, that was a kind of *coup de grâce* for the *It's a Wonderful Life* image of the local bank with the heart of gold, and it wasn't long before Leeds marketing consultant Michael Howard hit the media. He was the unhappy recipient of a new £20 overdraft charge for a £10 overdraft, that same year. After making the sort of reasonable request to have it lifted (which might have been complied with in past years) turned down, and feeling somewhat aggrieved, he changed his name by deed poll to Mr Yorkshire Bank PLC Are Fascist Bastards. The bank responded by saying he should close his account, which Mr Bastards was only too eager to do, provided they sent him a cheque for the remaining balance of 69 pence, made out in his new name.

In 2012 the National Bank of Australia announced a strategic review of its UK businesses, which resulted in the streamlining of its services, closing down many branches, with the loss of 1,400 jobs. Dear old Akroyd must be revolving in his grave.

JOHN NOAKES GETS DOWN ABOUT SHEP

1987

John Noakes, the longest-serving *Blue Peter* presenter, stunned the nation in 1987 when he appeared on the BBC programme *Fax!*, which featured answers to questions posed by its viewers. He was there to respond to the enquiry, 'Whatever happened to John Noakes and Shep?' The bluff, energetic and very Yorkshire Yorkshireman, icon for a whole generation with his fearless stunts and northern tones, wept openly on camera as he spoke of Shep's recent death. Shep, a lively border collie, was the pet assigned to John Noakes as part of the show, and the pair caught the hearts of millions with their adventures and escapades. Shep got in the way of everything, and John's remonstrance became a national catchphrase, delivered with varying degrees of ability to imitate the Yorkshire accent. The Barron Knights even wrote a song about the pair, a faux country and western send-up entitled, 'Get Down, Shep!'

Blue Peter, the BBC children's magazine programme, now heading towards its 5,000th show, provided many a seminal memory for those of us who were raised to focus on a mere three channels. There was the sticky-backed-plastic-tastic craft section, which offered a seemingly endless variety of things to do with a cornflakes packet and a Fairy Liquid bottle; the annual advent calendar made of tinsel and coat hangers; the baby elephant that pooed in the studio and offered gleeful children in 1969 a chance to see their hero, Noakes, falling about in faeces; not to mention the time when the *Blue Peter* garden was vandalised and the great Percy Thrower talked to the children of Britain as if he was our own betrayed grandad, instilling in those who had never applied a boot to a plant pot, nor even been to London, an abiding sense of guilt over the damage. I myself am the proud owner of a *Blue Peter* badge, which I got for drawing a picture of the show's new puppy; although I can't say that I go to pet shows very often, I bask in the knowledge that this coveted token of achievement, for a masterful creation with crayons, would still get me in for free.

The idea of having pets on the programme came about in the early 1960s, under the ethos of giving those children without animals of their own a collective feeling of ownership along with the show. In a charming festive episode, the head of children's TV appeared with a large present, and when the ribbons were released a tiny mongrel puppy stuck its nose out – and everybody got a puppy for Christmas! The fact that this puppy died of distemper two days later was only revealed in long-time producer Biddy Baxter's recent book, *Dear Blue Peter*. To 'protect' the nation's children from undue suffering, she and a colleague had dived into a mini and pelted round London like Starsky and Hutch, scouring pet shop windows to find a similar-looking mongrel to replace the unfortunate whelp before the next show. No one was any the wiser, quite literally, as a large part of the point of children having pets involves coming to terms with the fact that creatures die. This wasn't something *Blue Peter* were prepared to deal with on screen until 2004, when octogenarian George, the tortoise, passed away.

The sight of John Noakes abandoning himself to grief on national television was viewed with awkwardness by many outside the county, who saw it as an exception to the perceived rule of the Yorkshire temperament. At the time he presented *Blue Peter*, regional accents were still very rare in television and beside the cut-glass tones of fellow Blue Peterites Valerie Singleton and Peter Purves, the broad vowels and dropped t's, the lack of commencing h's and the strident intonation stuck out a north-of-Watford mile. But it would be a challenge to find a Yorkshireman who didn't see in Noakes' tears a perfectly comprehensible, nay familiar, part of the Yorkshire temperament. Dogs are the accepted emotional transmitters in households where not much is said of the sentimental sort, and their unspoken comprehension of the feelings we don't wish to discuss is highly valued. Many a Yorkshire child has seen a stoical father break down over the grave of man's best friend, while remaining

Sahara-eyed in the face of other life-shattering experiences. Truth is, up here we don't like to be expected to talk about things or show things we all know are there. We can go for a walk on the moors with a friend and barely say a word for the duration, or we can go for a walk with only our dog and talk to it incessantly. My father is not one for displays of affection towards the family. The love is not in doubt, but it is never manifested in hugs or blandishments. Picture the scene as I descended one morning to catch him showing our border collie old brown photographs and telling her, 'This was me when I was a puppy.'

In 2008 Noakes appeared on the special edition of *The Weakest Link* devoted to the world's longest-running children's programme and became visibly distressed again over a question relating to Shep. He was voted off as the second weak link, but his link to the complex personality of our county remained very much intact.

PIERREPOINT
1992

In 1916, at the age of 11, a West Yorkshire lad sat down in his English lesson to complete the task. He began, 'When I leave school I should like to be the Official Executioner …' Unlike the many wannabe astronauts, engine drivers and vets this old, worn exercise brings forth, and apart from the fact that there was no such title in the English penal system, that's just what he became. After conducting between 400 and 600 executions, with all the gravitas and efficiency that he became famous for, Albert Pierrepoint did indeed became Britain's 'official executioner' in the eyes of the people.

Albert was raised in Clayton near Huddersfield. His father and his uncle were both executioners, and he wanted to join the family trade. He read his uncle's diaries avidly whenever he was permitted and practised the rudiments of a neat, quick drop with a sack and a rope in the family barn. Albert was a perfectionist and applied himself to the science of weight-to-height ratios, as well as to the psychology of a condemned man. His first application to the Prison Commissioners in 1931 was rejected, but when a vacancy became available, he was summoned to interview at Strangeways Prison in Manchester and then to a week's training at Pentonville. He began as an assistant, earning three guineas a time, which infrequently supplemented his regular income as a grocer, before becoming a chief executioner and earning a much higher fee. The work was irregular and necessitated the utmost discretion. Pierrepoint didn't even mention it to his new wife, Annie Fletcher, until they had been together for some time, although Annie had already worked out his 'other career' for herself.

It was after the Second World War that Pierrepoint became something of a celebrity. The numerous war trials, conducted by British authorities investigating the atrocities of the concentration camps, handed down a large number of death sentences, and Albert was commissioned to carry them out. He travelled to Germany 25 times between 1945 and 1949, executing over 200 war criminals in his inimitable style – swift and civilised, a far cry from the recent execution of Saddam Hussein. 'Whoever they are, whatever they've done, if I can give them respect and dignity at the last moment, that's my job and I come away satisfied,' said Albert, speaking on BBC Radio Merseyside in 1976. When the press got hold of his identity, he was held up as a hero, bringing the Nazis to justice. He hanged commanders from Belsen and Auschwitz, names that struck fear into the hearts of many who had lost loved ones in the war. He also executed Bruno Tesch, inventor of Zyklon B, the monstrous chemical compound used to such shocking effect in the gas chambers. The trials generated so much work for Albert that he was able to retire from the grocery trade and become a publican, first at the curiously named Help the Poor Struggler near Failsworth, and later at the Rose and Crown near Preston, the scene of a strange encounter.

One James Corbitt, who used to frequent the Pierrepoints' pub with his girlfriend, appeared without her one evening in November 1950 and, in a mood of unusual levity, got up and sang a duet with Albert. It later transpired that he had murdered his girlfriend that very evening, in a fit of jealous rage. So it was that Albert came to hang one of his own customers, with the same deadpan northern efficiency as he hanged anyone else, although it seems that this particular case helped him towards his future controversial opinion on capital punishment, which he expressed long after his retirement, in his autobiography, *Executioner: Pierrepoint*. 'I have come to the conclusion that executions solve nothing, and are only the antiquated relic of a primitive desire for revenge ...' This, from the man who had such a vast experience of the death penalty, and who held the record for the fastest execution – seven seconds, from leaving the condemned cell to the trapdoor opening – may seem strange, but Pierrepoint had hanged men who were later reprieved, such as Timothy Evans, the dupe of John Christie, and he had hanged many men, like James Corbitt, whose crimes were not premeditated and for whom the deterrent was utterly irrelevant.

Whatever his beliefs, he was good at his job, and respectful of men and women facing their final hour. 'They're walking into the unknown,' he said, 'and anyone who's walking into the unknown, well, I'll take my hat off to them.'

Albert himself headed for the unknown in 1992, dying peacefully in a nursing home in Southport at the age of 87.

THE GREAT YORKSHIRE PUDDING BOAT RACE

1995

'Picture yourself in a boat on a river, with tangerine trees and marmalade skies ...' So sang the Beatles in their psychedelic classic 'Lucy in the Sky with Diamonds' back in 1967. Thirty years later and artist Simon Thackray, of Brawby, had an equally outlandish vision one lazy, sunny Sunday in his local pub as staff sailed past, navigating their way between tables and docking great steaming plates of roast beef in front of hungry punters. What is a Sunday dinner without a Yorkshire pudding in a sea of gravy? This is a question that needs no answer, but Mr Thackray pictured a Yorkie on the real sea, rather than gravy – and, with him inside it and before the millennium was out, the first Great Yorkshire Pudding Boat Race took place.

Yorkshire puddings have travelled the world without the aid of a paddle. They came into being as dripping puddings, a means of catching fat from the joint in a dripping pan, to which the simple batter was added. The dish was given its proper title in 1747 by Hannah Glasse in her classic book, *The Art of Cookery Made Plain and Simple,* and the rest, as they say, is history. Traditionally eaten before the main course in Yorkshire, as a way to fill up a hungry family on cheaper ingredients, they are now a long-acknowledged part of the classic roast dinner nationwide. An official ruling by the British Chemistry Society states that to qualify as authentic, a Yorkshire pudding has to rise to a height of four inches. This has scared many outside the county into attempting quack production methods, such as the unpardonable sin of using self-raising flour or the last-chance-saloon of the frozen variety. The effects are disastrous, a long way from the glorious crispy shell and soft golden interior that makes the Yorkshire so delicious. Having the same composition as pancake batter, it is customary for children to eat leftover puddings with syrup or jam, but then again, leftovers are a bit of a rarity!

Did an unsteady waitress's hand impart a 'bobbing' motion to the Yorkshire pudding that sailed past Simon Thackray on its sea of gravy? Something must have given him the idea. There are many wacky races at the eccentric end of the nautical calendar's spectrum: there's pumpkin racing in Ontario, where cavernous vegetables are hollowed out and motors attached; the Darwin Beercan Regatta in Australia, where some of the nation's favourite drink receptacles are recycled into ships of steel; and the American Society of Civil Engineers' annual concrete canoe championships, to name but a few. The Yorkshire pudding boat race involves considerable baking skill before one gets to the sailing stage, and quite a pile of ingredients, which has caused some to criticise the waste of good food. It's not a dainty recipe, with fifty eggs, four bags of flour and twenty-five pints of milk per pudding, but a good one lasts a fair while and might keep the sailor well fed if he veered sufficiently off course as to end up on a desert island. The pudding boats are made watertight with several coats of yacht varnish (not so palatable) after being baked in the oven.

So, each June the fleets line up on the noble shores of Bob's Pond in Brawby, near Malton, and set sail when the starter gives the order. Round boats made of anything are not the easiest things to manoeuvre, so it is perhaps for the best that there appears to be no finishing line of any kind.

A CALENDAR THAT SAW OFF
THE OLD MILLENNIUM
1999

Picture for a moment the idyll of rural village life in North Yorkshire. Lanes lined with mossy dry-stone walls undulating between watercolour cottages and barns, a pub where the landlord's dog knows everyone, a duck pond, a village shop, a café piled high with home-made cakes and rock buns, proper tea in proper teapots and all the worthy village women stark naked ...

In 1999, the Rylstone and District chapter of the Women's Institute came up with a unique variation on the 'tracks trickling with sheep' and 'barn door with bluebells' tradition of photographs for their annual charity calendar, one that would rocket them to fame across the globe and see the nationwide membership of the WI swell in years to come. Like all the best recipes, it was simple and original with a refreshing twist of a special ingredient – twelve tastefully composed sepia images of middle-aged respectable women represented in traditional scenes of pastoral domestic splendour, and not a stitch of clothing on any of them. All the usual paraphernalia associated with the very British bastion of the Women's Institute – the jam pan, the flower arrangement, a well-knitted sleeve or a perfectly executed Victoria sponge sandwich – were to provide the necessary cover for the scarcely conceivable nipples and muffs of these demure village ladies.

This unassailably tasteful send-up of the garage-wall style Pirelli calendar nudes was conceived as a fundraiser for leukaemia research after Angela Baker, an active member of the group, lost her husband John to the disease in 1998. How this idea went from a suggestion to a possibility to actually being executed, who knows, but it's fun to imagine that maybe the home-made wine created by the Rylstone WI members could have catalysed the project. There was some resistance to the idea of course, and approval had to be sought from national headquarters, but somehow all obstacles were surmounted and the photographs were taken, including a festive finale for December with all eleven women wearing nothing but Santa hats and holding carol sheets at strategic altitudes. The calendar was to go on sale for five pounds a pop and the ladies hoped its refreshing format would tweak up sales to around the £2,000 mark for their cause. The response turned out to be phenomenal. It sold more than double the number of Pirelli calendars that year – 88,000 flew off the shelves in the UK alone and an astounding 200,000 copies worldwide.

Unexpectedly, the calendar also generated thousands of letters from older women up and down the country who found the portrayals of their peers (the eldest calendar girl was 66) to be an inspiration, a restorative for their sagging self-esteem. Still more unexpected were the number of letters they received from men expressing appreciation at what the calendar had done for their wives. It came as a good kick in the pants of the old millennium, highlighting the developments in longevity and freedom for women well past 40 and their right to continue being beautiful and sensual as well as home-makers, jam-makers, tear-wipers and grandmothers. The ensuing public attention brought invitations for radio and television appearances, signings at bookshops and even an American tour after sales of their calendar beat Britney Spears' own contribution to illustrating the months of that year. Then Hollywood came to town, adapting the story into an award-winning film, *Calendar Girls*, in 2003 starring Helen Mirren and, of course, Julie Walters.

To date, the Rylstone and District chapter of the Women's Institute have been able to donate a whacking £2,000,000 to Leukaemia Research for their wonderful calendar and its spin-offs.

TWIN TOWNS
NOT SO FAR APART AS
THEY MAY SEEM
2001

Twin towns became popular after the Second World War, encouraging unity and understanding between neighbouring European countries. The first recorded English twinning agreement was between the West Yorkshire town of Keighley and Poix-du-Nord in France. They established a link in 1920, and the practice later became widespread. Nowadays they are commonly associated with visiting groups of teenagers, divided among the dinner tables of the school community, struggling to comprehend the baffling regional accents of enthusiastic parents and gazing aghast at mysterious local delicacies. They also equip our young people with a fascinating insider view of a foreign household and its customs, which will stay with them, like a vivid dream, until the end of their days. Twinning was often established between places with something in common: Coventry, Dresden and the former Stalingrad were connected by their shared suffering of severe wartime bombing; Oxford is twinned with other seats of learning, and so on. This is the tale of an unmarked and unofficial sort of twinning between Bradford and Mirpur in Pakistan.

There has been conflict in recent years between extreme factions from the white-British and Asian-British communities of Bradford. The Bradford Riots in July 2001 were catalysed by confrontations between the National Front and British National Party and the Anti-Nazi League. Trouble escalated over a period of days and involved around a thousand youths. There were attacks on shops, cars and other property. In the aftermath 200 prison sentences were handed down, amounting to a dizzying total of 604 years of jail. The damage estimate for the period was around £7 million and the Ouseley Report that was commissioned in its aftermath offered 67 recommendations to bring harmony to the city.

The Channel 4 documentary *Make Bradford British,* in which white people from the city were 'twinned' with people of colour, begins with 100 Bradford folk sitting the 'Life in the UK' test, an examination made up of questions that a person applying for citizenship status in this country would be expected to be able to answer. The spectacular failure of nearly all concerned to score even a basic pass mark was a unifying, illustrative starting point for the complex experience the participants underwent in learning about each other.

Bradford is the city at the centre of the municipal borough of Bradford; Mirpur is the main city of the Mirpur province. Bradford became a municipal borough in the late 1840s, when Mirpur became part of the new state of Jammu and Kashmir. They are both in hilly regions, set just over 400 metres above sea level, and both had flourishing industries related to water. Bradford grew into a major industrial centre for cloth manufacture, due to its abundance of soft water for washing wool and its proximity to coal supplies. Mirpur became a major trading centre on the busy Jhelum River, with its nearby rich forests facilitating boat building. In the mid-1900s both were dramatically changed by foreign intervention. Mirpur lost most of its residential and agricultural areas, which were submerged by the building of a gigantic reservoir, the Mangla Dam, one of the largest in the world and an American/British project. Bradford received a huge influx of immigrant workers to fill its booming post-war factories. The majority of these people had been displaced by the construction work in Mirpur. When they lost their agricultural land, many joined a scheme that offered them work in Britain, a circumstance very similar to the migration away from agriculture that had occurred in Britain's Industrial Revolution. The landscape of Mirpur altered dramatically, as had that of Bradford, which in Victorian times had over 200 mill chimneys belching out enough smoke to make it the most polluted city in the country at that time.

Nowadays both are multicultural cities that attract shoppers from around the region. Bradford is awaiting completion of the new Westfield shopping complex; Mirpur awaits the new Nosha shopping complex. Both are currently under construction. Most investment in the Mirpur economy these days is in the leisure and retail area, with shops such as the Bradford Shoe Shop, Topman Tailors and London Travel. Bradford is well known for its selection of Asian cuisine. With around 13 per cent of the population of Bradford being descendants of Mirpur, and a similar percentage of residences in Mirpur belonging to families from Bradford, the area has come to be nicknamed 'Bradistan' and Mirpur is 'Little England'. Apart from the indisputable fact that the climates could not be more different, I can't help wondering why these two cities, with so much – from history to community – in common, have never been officially twinned.

THE RETURN OF THE HARTLEPOOL MONKEY?
2005

In 2005, something washed up on the beach at Hartlepool that caused a bit of a stir, rekindling an old tale for which this formerly Yorkshire town became famous.

It was back in the time of the Napoleonic Wars, when residents of Yorkshire's east coast were living in fear of invasion, or at the very least infiltration of their communities by French spies. Great ships of the French fleet were occasionally seen passing at a distance and this fuelled these concerns. On one particular occasion, fishermen watched a tempest-tossed French ship battling for survival not far off the coast of their native Hartlepool, and although relieved when the vessel foundered and sank, they maintained their vigil in case any survivors should sneak ashore. Raking through the wreckage that began to wash up along the shoreline, they discovered one very bedraggled and sopping individual, the like of which they had never seen before. He was very small in stature and very hairy, with a full facial beard, not to mention tufts sprouting from the ankles and cuffs of his Napoleonic naval uniform, and it seems he may even have had a useful-looking tail. He failed to identify himself, or to respond to their questions with anything but gibberish. With these alien characteristics, what else could he be but a Frenchman!

The fishermen raised the alarm and hastily assembled an impromptu court, right there and then, made up of fishing specialists rather than the more traditional legal personnel, who, to be fair, would probably have been in short supply on the beach that day. Neither was likely to get much sense out of a monkey, dressed for the amusement of a ship's crew in a miniature version of their uniform, but they had never seen a real Frenchman before and didn't know what to expect. The 'leetle fellow' was found guilty of intention to spy for the enemy, sentenced to death by hanging, and a convenient nearby fishing coble lent its mast for a gibbet, thus extending the nautical metaphor of these peculiar legal proceedings right through to the execution itself.

What a day for the poor old monkey: half-drowned, before being shouted at by his apparent saviours, and then lynched by a terrifying mob. He had his retribution in the succeeding years, as word of the incident got round the neighbouring towns, and 'monkey hangers' became for some time a common term of abuse for Hartlepudlians (yes, Hartlepudlians!). Shouts of 'Who hanged the monkey?' developed into a common means of riling inhabitants of the little coastal town. As time went by, however, this ceased to be derogatory as the people of the town became prouder of their history and defended the home-guard enthusiasm of those patriotic fishermen. Their rugby union team, Hartlepool Rovers, are known affectionately as 'the Monkeyhangers' and a monkey named H'Angus stands as the mascot for their football club.

No one really knows whether or not the story is true, but it lives on in the hearts of local people as gospel. There are some suggestions that the monkey may have been a French boy, referencing the old slang 'powder monkeys' as a term for children kept aboard ships to scuttle around priming cannons with gunpowder. Who knows?

Hartlepudlians seem to be somewhat susceptible to the monkey mystery even now, whether or not the tale is mere legend. A large bone was washed ashore in 2005 and picked up from Hartlepool beach by a local resident. Much excitement surrounded this event. Surely, this was proof at last of the monkey's existence? Alas, no. The bone underwent analysis and scientists identified it as belonging to a red deer. The fact that it was a 6,000-year-old red deer was some consolation, and it is now exhibited at The Museum of Hartlepool.

KEEPING THE KINE IN THE DARK
2008

Scammonden is a remote Pennine area of great natural beauty and although, like everywhere else in Yorkshire these days, it has suffered some of the sanitising influence of comers-in turning the Nativity-esque magic of old hay barns into draught-free spotless residences, much of it holds out against 'progress'. Local milk farmers, defending themselves, have had to see off court cases brought by newcomers who complain that the lowly cattle are incontinent as they plod down lanes from milking to pasture, and that this is soiling their shiny new gateposts or spoiling their 'got-the-barn, got-the-Range-Rover' notions of country life. In 2008 a similar piece of lunacy occurred, showing how the grip of modern Health and Safety terrorism has tightened, leaving nowhere safe from reactionary state interference.

A Scammonden smallholder became the subject of some bizarre proceedings after a routine inspection visit to check his kine – an old Yorkshire word for cattle – for tuberculosis. The cows, all one and a half of them, tested clear and the inspectors, not content, asked to be shown where the cow and calf were kept in winter. They slept in a barn set into the hillside, beneath the old Co-op building, where farmer Ronald Norcliffe has lived for most of his life. Both Kirklees environmental health police and DEFRA (the Department for Environmental Food and Rural Affairs) were horrified at there being no electric light in the barn, and learning that the door was kept closed at night to keep the cows warm, leaving only a small window for light to seep through, had them practically bellowing for their smelling salts. It cannot be anything new to the average Yorkshire cow that in winter it is dark by four o'clock, but the fact that Mr Norcliffe seemed unmoved by the distress of officials at his cows' apparent suffering, and remained unwilling to do anything to make them feel better about it, led to a charge of 'failing to meet the psychological and ethological needs' of his cow.

Literacy is an important issue these days. Children who are read bedtime stories at home benefit significantly in literacy terms. So I suppose it's understandable that if Daisy cannot read to her poor calf in the long winter evenings, how can it hope to have a fighting chance of competent literacy in adult life? What are the ethological and psychological needs of a cow, and how are those needs being met in DEFRA-approved slaughterhouse trucks?

Scammonden is timelessly beautiful and if I were one of the dumb beasts in question, an old-fashioned barn, with my calf by my side, wouldn't sound like a poor lot compared to that of modern cattle amid the bright lights and clanking of production-line farming. Unlike Hannah Hauxwell, who became the 1970s heroine of many a documentary as a Daleswoman farming in anachronistic rusticity, Mr Norcliffe was dragged through court in his flat cap and overalls and fined for his 'cruelty', no irony at all being spotted in his having no electricity in his own farmhouse either. He is a product of a simpler age, and has lived with nothing after dark but a fire and candles all his life.

FATAL DELUSIONS

2009

On 31 August 2009, a man threw himself off the North Bridge Flyover in Halifax. Witnesses at the scene clearly heard him laughing as he fell. It was his second jump from the same spot where he had also tried to end his life in 1994, hours after murdering his mother. This time he succeeded.

This is the awful tale of psychotic Stewart Dawson, who developed an obsession with the Old Testament in his early twenties, interpreting it in a very unbalanced way. Somehow he had become increasingly convinced that his 52-year-old mother Angela was a dragon or some sort of vessel of Satan. This notion grew and grew until one day he dispatched her at their family home with repeated blows from a frying pan – 14 to be precise. He then headed for the bridge to take his own life. It wasn't the last he was to see of the frying pan, as he survived the 60-foot fall and returned home. Hard as it is to imagine, Dawson put the pan to even more sinister use before his mother was discovered to be missing.

The police were alerted by concerned members of the public, who had seen the young man fall, survive, and leave the scene in a stunned state. This, added to further witness reports identifying Dawson wandering in local gardens, burning tracts from the Bible and carrying a handful of raw meat, led officers to pay him a visit. On entering the house, the police found grizzly evidence of Dawson's very troubled state of mind; it was one of the most shocking crime scenes of the twentieth century. They found the remains of his mother stuffed under the bed. He had disembowelled her and gouged out her eyes, and she was also missing an arm and a leg. The family dog had been throttled too and its tongue was cut out. What was found cooking on the stove must have haunted the dreams of those police officers for years, never mind those of Mr Dawson. Amid a litter of scribbled biblical quotations, a collection of pentagrams, crucifixes and other religious icons, Dawson had turned cannibal.

Stewart Dawson was convicted of manslaughter and secured in Rampton high-security mental hospital, where he remained for some time and received treatment for schizophrenia. He was released in 2001, first to Newton Lodge secure psychiatric hospital in Wakefield and later, at his own request, into the care of his GP. For several years he lived independently in Huddersfield and had a girlfriend who knew nothing of his history. When they broke up, the local medical practice noticed Dawson's failure to attend the fortnightly appointment for his risperidone anti-psychotic injection, a condition of his release, and notified his GP. Still, no one went to check up on the whereabouts of Stewart Dawson.

Taking into account the extremely disturbed history of this unstable young man, it seems strange that no alarm was raised; even stranger that this troubled soul was released, and stranger still that he was allowed to regulate his own medical treatment. Taking the hands-off approach to extremes, he had not been visited by a community nurse since 2008. At the inquest into the death of Dawson, medical staff refused to offer any comment on the situation, saying only that they were required to act within the guidelines of their professional roles and that they were bound by confidentiality not to discuss a patient's case with third parties.

Before we are too hasty to pass judgement on Dawson for the shocking murder of his mother, it should be remembered that he had no control over his condition and that in his subsequent un-medicated state, 15 years later, the only person he harmed was himself.

GANNEX MILL IS
PULLED DOWN
2011

The demolition of Gannex Mill, one of Calderdale's best-known landmarks, was completed early in 2011, marking the end of the strange history of its owners, Lord and Lady Kagan. Lord Joseph Kagan was a millionaire tycoon whose well-known product, the Gannex raincoat, was famously adopted by Harold Wilson as he rose to political prominence in the 1950s. It then became popular attire on both sides of the Cold War, worn by US President Lyndon Johnson as well as Russian Premier Nikita Kruschev. The Queen and Prince Philip sported them, so did the corgis in typically inclement British weather, and the Gannex remained an essential item in the luggage of the Jet Set for many years. The same fabric was worn on Arctic and Antarctic expeditions and by the police. Even Mao Tse-tung wore a Gannex coat, incredible as it sounds. In fact, the geographical and political proliferation of this garment tends to suggest that there was undoubtedly a serious gap in the market for a really good-quality weatherproof in the 1950s, and Joseph Kagan spotted it.

This popular and flamboyant figure experienced a fall from grace in 1980 and was imprisoned for 10 months for tax evasion. He was relieved of his knighthood, but retained his peerage, awarded in Wilson's infamous Resignation Honours List, and continued to speak eloquently on socialist issues in the House of Lords after his release. Kagan died in 1995, survived by his widow Margaret, who at the age of 85 went along to watch the bulldozers close in on the family's massive mill in Elland. This much of their lives is well known; the rest of their history reads like a film script – they were successful, yes, but they went through hell to get there.

To borrow a cliché, Lady Margaret Kagan was the great woman behind her great man. She had an enormous passion for life and an indomitable spirit. She spoke seven languages fluently and intelligently, and always with a keen sense of humour. Her life was defined by humanitarian ideals and she spoke out against persecution and social injustice. Not without good reason: she was born in the 1920s in Riga, Latvia, to a Russian mother and Lithuanian father, both non-observing Jews. Her father was an economic adviser to the Lithuanian Embassy at that time and they later moved back to Lithuania. Margaret was just a teenager when the Nazis invaded the Soviet Union in 1941 and although many Jews fled, her family did not. Her younger brother was away at a children's holiday camp and unable to just abandon him, they stayed in the Kaunas ghetto, with disastrous consequences.

Margaret's family were nearly all killed in the Holocaust. Her father one day went out to hand in his business keys and never returned. He was one of many Jewish men who were beaten to death in the infamous Lietukis Garage massacre. Margaret's mother was deported to Stutthof Concentration Camp in Poland, where she survived for only four months. Margaret met an unusual young man in the ghetto: Joseph, who was part of a slave-labour brigade. He refused to ignore the ominous signs that they would all eventually be murdered and, with the help of a non-Jewish factory owner, secretly worked on building a hiding place for that eventuality. Margaret married Joseph at 17. In 1943 she and her husband and new mother-in-law were given refuge by their brave friend, who risked his life walling them up, Anne Frank-style, in the nine-foot box Joseph had constructed in the attic of the factory, just over the wall from the ghetto. Not much of a honeymoon, and a far cry from Wordsworth's 'daffodils' house, Eusemere, in the Lake District, which the couple were to later own. They survived in hiding for nine months as thousands perished around them. At the end of the war, they managed to escape to Britain, a journey that took over a year.

Their clothing empire had modest beginnings – a Nissen hut and a dizzying business start-up capital totalling eight pounds. They worked hard. Joseph invented the Gannex waterproof fabric (consisting of a layer of nylon, an air gap, and a layer of wool), and by 1959 they had bought the Gannex Mill and employed a thousand people from the local area. The Kagans became part of Harold Wilson's inner circle and were often featured in the press calling for social reform.

After his stint inside for tax evasion, Joseph campaigned for an improvement in prison standards (no doubt with the mirthless walls of his recent home, Armley Gaol, in mind). It's quite a testament that the public in general were inclined to be rather more forgiving of his crime than one would normally expect, and seemed to excuse this man who had been through such horrors and worked so hard to the general benefit of his Yorkshire community. The Kagans were decent folk, who remained so after they became very rich.

Lady Kagan spent much of her life working for Holocaust survivors and championing other humanitarian causes. She managed to get back to Eastern Europe to meet and thank the factory owner, Vytautas Rinkevicius, who had risked his own and his family's lives to hide Margaret and her husband in 1943.

It is hard to adequately portray a woman like Margaret. She lived modestly after her husband died, among the Yorkshire people with whom she felt so at home. Even in her eighties she looked both cool and down-to-earth, wearing leather pants. That's quite an achievement in one's eighties, but the Kagans were always stylish. Lady Kagan was not above thumbing a lift or chatting on the local bus, even though they had once owned a plane, and she still had her pilot's licence. She received a ticking-off, however, for using her own distinctive method of navigating Yorkshire: swooping low to check the colours of the buses in order to find her way home. It was just that pragmatic and spirited approach to life which made her who she was. The Kagans had found the Wordsworth house for sale on one of their flights over the Lake District and, complete with jetty, they bought it as their family holiday home. Every year the disadvantaged children of Calderdale were invited to stay there too, for a summer camp.

Lady Margaret Kagan survived the Gannex Mill by only a couple of months, having suffered with lung cancer for some time. She was buried in her beloved Yorkshire after a funeral in Huddersfield Town Hall attended by people from all over the globe, who paid tribute to the many ways she had helped them, describing her as a remarkable woman of intelligence, and a humanitarian of great value. Not a bad epitaph for anyone.

GOD'S OWN COUNTY
GOES GOLD
2012

Yorkshire has long regarded itself as worthy of being a country in its own right, and the people of Yorkshire are known for having a greater loyalty to their county than to Britain as a whole. Yorkshire covers a huge area: West Yorkshire alone is the second largest county in the land, and despite its official depletion over the years, through governments chopping and whittling at its edges, the sporting and regimental boundaries are still intact, along with the historic boundaries in the hearts of the people. The great summer of sport occasioned by the Olympic Games being hosted in London offered the opportunity for an upsurge in the general enthusiasm of Yorkshire men and women for God's Own County, as it is affectionately known. If Yorkshire had been a country, it would have finished 12th overall in the ranking for the summer Olympics 2012!

The county is no newcomer to sporting success. Yorkshire County Cricket holds a total of 30 championship titles, which puts it 12 ahead of any other county. It was also the only cricket club to hold out against the 1968 reforms that other clubs adopted, allowing them to field players from anywhere in the world. Yorkshire stuck by the principle of only recruiting players who were born within its historic county boundaries until 1992, when it amended the rule slightly to include those educated within the county as well. Add to this pedigree England's oldest horse race, at Kiplingcotes, which began in 1519 and is still running (the horses must be getting very tired); the first football club, Sheffield FC, which was founded in 1857 and is the oldest in the world; and the birth of Rugby League, which was founded in 1895 in the George Hotel in Huddersfield.

Olympic fever began early, with towns and villages flocking to cheer on the flaming torch procession, and high hopes for the many top-flight athletes the county fields. Success was ensured in some measure by Yorkshire's track record, 'The Tykes' having carried home 23 per cent of Britain's medals from Beijing in 2008. As the games progressed, a Yorkshire radio sports reporter, Jonathan Buchan, spring-boarded speculation on White Rose's performance as a nation when he tweeted in early August that if Yorkshire was a country, it would currently be ranked 11th. This observational gem was re-tweeted more than 3,000 times and the tabloids took up the story with 'Ee bah gum!' headlines and suggestions of something in the water, the beer or the gravy, but we could tell they were impressed as Yorkshire surged ahead of Japan, Brazil and a little place called Australia. To clarify Yorkshire's secret, Nicola Adams, who became the first woman boxer ever to win in an Olympics, declared it must have been down to all the Yorkshire puddings. At its zenith in the guise of an actual nation, the county made it to 9th place before slipping back a little. Seven gold medals, two silvers and three bronzes later, the crowds, and the Yorkshire Tourist Board, were going wild. The Republic of Yorkshire finished 12th overall. Not a bad performance at all.

If Yorkshire was a country? *If*? There are more than a few among its 5 million residents, myself included, who firmly believe that the land of the White Rose has never been anything else.

BIBLIOGRAPHY

BOOKS

Balston, Thomas, *The Life of Jonathan Martin with some account of William and Richard Martin* (Macmillan, 1945)

Carrington, Charles, *The Life of Rudyard Kipling* (Doubleday, 1955)

Flanders, Judith, *A Circle of Sisters: Alice Kipling, Georgiana Burne-Jones, Agnes Poynter, and Louisa Baldwin* (Penguin Books, 2002)

Gillies, Midge, *Amy Johnson: Queen of the Air* (Weidenfeld & Nicolson, 2003)

Green, Jeffrey, *Black Edwardians: Black People in Britain 1901–1914* (Routledge, 1998)

Sobel, Dava, *Longitude* (Fourth Estate, 1996)

Wilson, Prof. David, *A History of British Serial Killing* (Sphere, 2011)

Wynne, William A., *Yorkie Doodle Dandy: A Memoir* (Wynnesome Press, 1996)

MAGAZINES

Green, J., 'Edwardian Britain's Forest Pygmies' (*History Today*, Vol. 45, Iss. 8).

WEBSITES

Discoveringyorkshire.org
Myyorkshire.org

Created in 2007, Portico publishes a range
of books that are fresh, funny and forthright.

PORTICO

An imprint of **Anova** Books

WROTTEN ENGLISH

A Celebration of Literary Misprints, Mistakes and Mishaps

Peter Haining

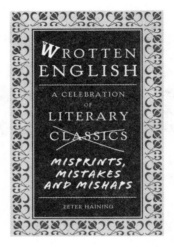

'An absolute gem of a book'

booksmonthly.co.uk

Following on from the hilarious collection of typos, gaffes and howlers in Portico's *A Steroid Hit the Earth*, comes *Wrotten English* – a fabulously funny collection of literary blunders from classic, and not-so classic, works of literature. This book is an anthology of side-splitting authors' errors, publishers' boobs, printers' devils, terrible titles, comical clangers and all manner of literary lunacy dating back since the invention of the printing press.

£9.99 • Hardback • 9781907554100

365 REASONS TO BE CHEERFUL

Magical Moments to Cheer Up Miserable Sods ...
One Day at a Time

Richard Happer

It's a well-observed fact that human beings can be a grumpy old bunch, always choosing to see that infamous metaphorical glass as constantly half empty rather than half full. Where's the fun in that? *365 Reasons To Be Cheerful* is, well, it's exactly that. It's a whole year's worth of funny and unique events that happened on each and every day – a wild, weird and wonderful journey through the year highlighting the moments that changed the world for the better as well as the delightfully quirky stories that will simply make you smile. 365 Reasons To Be Cheerful is designed specifically to look on the bright side of life every day of the year – the perfect pint-sized pick-me-up in these sobering, sombre times.

£7.99 • Hardback • 9781906032968

THE STRANGEST SERIES

9781861052933

9781861055354

9781861052926

9781861051844

9781905798285

9781861059765

9781906032906

9781907554131

9781861054111

9781905798162

9781861057457

9781861056795

9781861058270

9781907554339

9781861059383

9781907554971